Praise for *The Power of Belief*

"*The Power of Belief* is an incredible treasure, a deeply insightful model of awareness and change."

—Eric Sanderson, JD, LLM, Adjunct Professor of Law,
University of Denver

"I spent most of yesterday with *The Power of Belief.* It was a delightful day as I went cover to cover with eagerness for the next words. I enjoyed its simple and direct writing style and the clarity of the message. It left me inspired."

—Beverly Title, Ph.D., Teaching Peace, Boulder, Colorado

"This is a very powerful book, a practical roadmap to personal freedom. *The Power of Belief* is a loving reference, which I am sure will remain so for many years to come."

—Philip Jameson, LICSW, Psychotherapist, Rhode Island

"Much of what I learned from *The Four Agreements* has been deeply enhanced by *The Power of Belief.* I resonated with the examples and exercises, which bring the general to the specific. Sending boundless gratitude."

—Michele Laub, MS, Life Coach, Long Island, New York

The
POWER
Of BELIEF

ESSENTIAL TOOLS FOR AN EXTRAORDINARY LIFE

RAY DODD

HAMPTON ROADS
PUBLISHING COMPANY, INC.

Cover design by Steve Amarillo
Cover painting, "Freedom," by Diane Dandeneau

Hampton Roads Publishing Company, Inc.
1125 Stoney Ridge Road
Charlottesville, VA 22902

434-296-2772
fax: 434-296-5096
e-mail: hrpc@hrpub.com
www.hrpub.com

If you are unable to order this book from your local
bookseller, you may order directly from the publisher.
Call 1-800-766-8009, toll-free.

Library of Congress Cataloging-in-Publication Data
Dodd, Raymond, A., 1954-
    The power of belief : essential tools for an
extraordinary life/Ray Dodd
    p. cm.
    ISBN 0-97158636-5
    1.Conduct of life. 2. Toltec philosophy --
Miscellanea. 3. Belief and doubt. 4. Success --
Psychological aspects. I. Title.
BJ1595.D64 2004
299.7'9
                          QBI04-200049

ISBN 1-57174-404-5
10 9 8 7 6 5 4 3 2 1

Printed on acid-free paper in Canada

We don't see things as they are,
we see things as we are.

—Anaïs Nin

CONTENTS

INTRODUCTION

Belief is Power. The power to create. You create your own reality simply by what you agree to believe. Your deepest beliefs about everything hold your attention and propel you into action, or keep you from taking action. What you believe impacts your performance at work, your attitudes about money, how you navigate through the world, and how you conduct all your relationships.

Belief colors every experience and determines how we react in any situation, yet we are often unaware of the hidden beliefs that guide us. Sometimes our beliefs hold us back from realizing our deepest desires. Oftentimes it is the long-forgotten agreements we've made with ourselves that keep us stuck, repeatedly making choices in conflict with what we say we value most.

When you come to understand the real power of belief, you'll discover you have the ability to create any point of view you choose. Learn to exercise that power and you can defeat fear-based beliefs about yourself and the world around you that keep you from the inner peace and happiness you've always desired. Harness the power of belief and you'll break through self-limiting boundaries you were convinced could *never, ever* change.

In my practice as a life and workplace coach, I assist people who are motivated to change whatever is holding them back. They have already decided where they want to go, they're just not exactly sure how to get there. Traditional coaching focuses on what is true now, in the present moment, and what actions need to be taken to produce different results. However, mapping out strategies and taking action is only one piece of the puzzle.

While facilitating transformation for both individuals and organizations, I have noticed that focusing on what people believe is far more powerful than problem solving. Concentrating on what they believe has been vastly more effective than dissecting the stories they tell me and then working from the details. Many times working from the details creates managed solutions without the actual problem ever being resolved. In order to effect lasting and positive change, they need to change what they believe.

The Power of Belief, born out of hundreds of coaching sessions and my own experiences, and broadly influenced by both classical and contemporary philosophy, is deeply rooted in the ancient wisdom of the

Toltecs. In 1996 on a trip to the pyramid ruins in Teoti-huacán, Mexico, I had the good fortune to meet don Miguel Ruiz, author of the best-selling book about the teachings of the Toltec, *The Four Agreements*. Don Miguel is a former medical doctor and teacher dedicated to carrying on his family's spiritual heritage.

Not long after the trip, I began to study with don Miguel. I went to see him on a regular basis over a period of six years and those visits began a new chapter in my life.

Prior to meeting don Miguel, I spent many years trying to find a way to heal my own unhappiness and dissatisfaction. I was always looking for something different or better. I was addicted to identifying what was wrong with everything, so I tried whatever I could think of—moving to a new place, finding a different job, starting a new relationship—all with the potential to get me what I thought I needed. I went through portions of this cycle many times, buying into the myth that everything would be okay when I had this, or when I found that.

Having mixed results trying to change what was outside of me, I started on an inward journey that took me to many philosophies, faiths, and practices. I worked with various types of healers and read mountains of motivational and self-help books. I studied numerous spiritual traditions, had a martial arts practice in Aikido, and even spent time in a seminary.

Along the way I accumulated lots of wonderful

knowledge I wholeheartedly agreed with, yet I was still struggling, frequently overpowered by fear and emotional reactions to just about everything. At the time, I thought simply collecting all that information would do the trick. Looking back now, I realize I wasn't living all those ideas that sounded so good to me because I didn't really believe them.

My own process of change went into high gear when I began to study with don Miguel. Nothing he taught was in conflict with what I had learned up to that point. In fact, it complemented it. I discovered the Toltec way is unique, chock-full of simple yet brilliant devices that produce extraordinary results when put into practice. I have done my best to include as many as possible in this book.

The Toltecs were an ancient culture chiefly located in what is now the pyramid ruins of Teotihuacán in the high midlands of Mexico. In a tradition that dates back thousands of years and continues today, the Toltecs were known throughout Mexico as men and women of knowledge. One interpretation of the word "Toltec" is "artist." They considered the manner in which you lived your life as your art; thus the Toltec way was not a religion but more accurately a way of life.

The Toltec view embodies many universally accepted truths adopted by bona fide faiths and spiritual traditions around the world, along with a common-sense approach to explaining what we are and how we got this way. The Toltecs taught there is no way for us to change unless we have an awareness of how we create our own unique perception of the world. Their description of the human being is that the mind is alive, and one of its main purposes is to dream. They concluded we are dreaming twenty-four hours a day, and what we dream through is the filter of our beliefs about everything.

You are always modifying what you see, according to what you believe. What you believe produces a unique description of the world and drives most of your thoughts, your judgments, your joys, and your sorrows. It is very real, yet amazingly enough, it is only real for you and no one else.

My understanding of the Power of Belief began 25 years ago when I tried to quit smoking cigarettes. Although I only smoked a few cigarettes a day, I had come to despise the habit. About that time, the government began to force the cigarette manufacturers to publicize the health hazards of smoking and print warnings on the package. Even the pack of cigarettes said smoking was bad for you!

I had all the information I needed to make a decision to quit smoking, but I just couldn't stop. I would quit for a few days, buy a pack, smoke a few cigarettes, and then throw the pack away in disgust. I tried everything there was on the market to help me quit smoking. I bought nicotine gum, books, tapes, and took special supplements. I even tried hypnosis, but none of it helped. Sometimes I would quit for weeks. The physical addiction to the nicotine would subside, but something much more powerful was pulling me back into the habit. My level of frustration became enormous.

One night as I was drifting off to sleep I heard an unfamiliar voice from deep within me say, *You don't care whether you live or die.* I immediately dismissed the thought as preposterous. "Of course I care. I want to live!" I said to myself. But as the days passed I started to look carefully at this thought that had risen from a level well below what I was conscious of. *You don't care whether you live or die.* The words haunted me. When I stopped denying it, something emerged from me. I became aware of a hidden memory that now existed only as a long-forgotten dream. There was a part of me that believed exactly what I had discovered. It was true and yet it had been invisible to me. That awareness was startling and yet very powerful. Maybe I believed it, but I could no longer agree with it. The part of me that believed it was from another time in my life. Once I understood that, I stopped smoking immediately. The battle was over. It was never about smoking. It was all about what I had believed.

Whether you are aware of it or not, the entire tapestry of your life—woven together with the threads of belief—is your work of art. We are all Toltecs, artists of life. So whether you are interested in changing limited beliefs that stand in your way, increasing your communication skills by recognizing what others truly believe, or using the positive beliefs that have served you well as a springboard to the next level of personal achievement, the *Power of Belief* can be a very valuable tool.

Step by step, the *Power of Belief* illustrates how to remap any belief that is an obstacle to getting the results you want, unleashing the potential for profound transformation in every facet of your life.

The *Power of Belief* is divided into three sections. Part 1, "The First Dream," examines the ability we have to devise our own personal reality or dream. It defines what belief is, shows how our belief system was created, and describes how hidden beliefs can affect us in ways that no longer serve our best interests. Part 2, "The Second Dream," contains tools for redesigning the beliefs and agreements you want to change. Part 3, "Tools," includes a list of definitions for terms used throughout the book. Some of the terms are taken directly from the Toltec mythology, some I have modified from the original concepts, and some are my own invention.

Over the years I have noticed that what I considered a simple idea could be a maddening puzzle for my clients and students. They needed to hear it over and over again in lots of different forms before they would start to comprehend what was being said. Looking back over my own process, I did the very same thing. My teachers would repeat many times over concepts that are obvious to me now but certainly weren't then. These devices, the terms in the book, are designed to help you clearly understand the core ideas that are fundamental to grasping the Power of Belief.

It is awareness of the awesome force of belief that creates possibility. Possibility limited only by what you can imagine. Positive belief anchored in respect, love, gratitude, integrity, and self-acceptance provides you, the artist, with a new brush that makes bold strokes. It is time to create the life you've only dreamed of. But to do this you must be ready. Ready to change what you believe!

Part I

The First Dream

Chapter 1

THE FABRIC OF BELIEF

Belief is a living dream with volition, memory, dialog, agreements, and a distinct emotional point of view. Your beliefs are a series of filters you perceive through and, without awareness, they dream your life for you, whether you are awake or asleep.

I f you want to change your life—*Right Now*—there is nothing more powerful than changing what you believe!

Belief creates your personal reality: a unique world view where often what is true is true only for you. All the things you have experienced, everything anyone has ever said to you, and all the things you have ever read form a filter of belief through which you interpret everything. Its expression is the conversation you hear chattering in your mind—proclaiming how everything is, describing what you know, telling you about everything you believe.

The interpretation of life through the filter of belief alters what you perceive. Imagine you and I are looking at a dog. If you remember your high school biology, the light reflecting off the dog enters the retina in your eye and through a series of biochemical reactions, receptors process what you see, sending an electrical impulse to the brain and creating an image in your mind. The image is raw data. What you actually perceive is distorted by how you interpret the data.

What you observe is not actual but virtual. If I love dogs and you are afraid of dogs, we are each going to have a different experience. What you see and feel and what I see and feel are not exactly the same even though we are looking at the same dog. In a similar way, if a college art class is drawing a human model, the students don't all draw the same thing in the same way. Granted, some of this is because not everyone has the same level of skill or technique, but more importantly, the artists are expressing what they see inside their own virtual reality.

Most of the time we don't have any direct contact with what we perceive at all. Unless we are tasting something, or feeling the texture and temperature by touching it, our perception is derived largely from the image in our mind and the sounds we hear.

No one has a pure perception of the world they encounter moment to moment because we distort the information received by the senses based on past experience and our agreements about that experience. An example: If I invite you to dinner at my mother's house and she serves us my favorite dish, what you taste will likely be different from what I taste. Similarly, if you invite me to a concert where they are performing music you're familiar with, but I've never heard before, my experience is not going to be the same as yours.

To make matters worse, we distort the already altered version of reality presented to us by other people. To illustrate, let's say you are my friend. You know me and we have talked many times. You go to a party and get into a conversation with a man you've never met before. You tell the man about me but you don't give him my name. My sister goes to the same party and talks to the same man about me but also does not mention my name. By chance the very next day my mother runs into the same man in the supermarket and while they are waiting in the checkout line, she starts to tell him about her son. It is likely this man will think he was told about three different people because what he heard was how I existed in each of their minds. What he experienced was their perception of me through the lens of their agreements, opinions, and beliefs.

The typical understanding of belief is that it is a product of the mind, a condition produced by our reason. Something is true because we think it is true. We are under the impression that what we think we believe is actually what we believe. However, what we think we believe is often just an opinion. Opinions are not beliefs but the application of all the knowledge we have agreed to and our relentless defense of those agreements.

Beliefs are not solely a product of our thinking; in fact, they often animate our thinking. Belief is so much more than what we think is true. It's a product of all the human tools of perception and the evolution of what we have agreed to. What we believe is the result of all the long-forgotten oaths and promises we've made with ourselves.

Consider another definition for the word "belief." *Belief is a living dream with volition, memory, dialog, agreements, and a distinct emotional point of view. Your beliefs are a series of filters you perceive through, and without awareness they dream your life for you—whether you are awake or asleep.*

What you really believe is what you have no doubt about. Let's say you need to run an errand and you decide to drive your car to get there. You leave your house, walk out to the car, open the car with your keys, get in, put the key in the ignition, start the car, and begin to drive away. For most people, this whole sequence is pretty routine. You don't think much about it. You aren't considering how a key works in a lock or how the motor of a car operates after you turn the key. You don't consider it because you've done it many times, and you don't have any doubt about what will happen. It's not conscious, it's automatic. You believe it works. You believe it works because that is where you have invested your faith.

Where your faith is invested is powerful and very difficult to change just by changing your thinking. As an example, according to psychologists the greatest fear people have is not of dying but of speaking in front of other people. Many people have stage fright and so one way to overcome this fear is to take a public speaking course. A course like that can be very helpful, but what it really does is help manage fear. When they step out onto the stage, even after they've finished the course, there is often still something trying to overpower all the affirmations, techniques, and good intentions. That something is what they believe. That something is what they believe about themselves.

Many times our most deeply held beliefs are invisible to us. We think we know what we believe, but maybe we really don't. Ask yourself: What do I believe about money? What do I believe about work? What do I really believe about God, love, family, or the world around me? You can probably come up with some pretty good answers, but are they true? Suppose you tell everyone that you believe in being kind, considerate, and loving. What happens when someone doesn't act kind, considerate, and loving towards you? How do you feel when someone doesn't act kind or considerate towards someone you care about? When you are driving your car and another driver does something you don't like, is your reaction in conflict with what you told everyone you believed?

Belief can be so powerful that it controls your entire body. Just look in the mirror when you are upset or stressed. Look at your face and how you are holding your body. Notice whether your breathing is deep or shallow. Belief affects our biological systems too. There is much written about how fear, stress, and negative thinking can cause dis-ease in the human body. There is also lots of evidence on how love, positive thought, laughter, and touch aid in the healing of the same diseases.

Because belief lives below the level of ordinary awareness, you don't notice the agreements you made long ago. What you notice is the emotional point of view of the belief. When you are triggered by a stressful situation, what you're really aware of is being overwhelmed by the emotion. Even if you have learned to hold back your words, the reaction to what has happened or what has been said is far more powerful than any thought you might have about how you should or shouldn't act. It's a runaway train and you're not in control. In those moments, forcing yourself to behave in a way you think is acceptable can be like trying to strap down the lid on the pot so the water doesn't boil over while the flame underneath is turned all the way up.

Real transformation of the belief system cannot be accomplished simply by deciding to believe something else, reciting affirmations, or collecting more information. Have you ever been to a seminar, come back all fired up with lots of good information and the best intentions only to find months later that not much has really changed? We learn to talk the talk, but we can't seem to walk the walk. We can't seem to walk the walk because real transformation of the beliefs comes from engaging the totality of what we are. The totality of what we are created our beliefs and it is going to take all that to change them. We are so much more than just intellect and reason. We are vastly more than just our thinking. We are this human body with the senses of touch, sight, hearing, taste, and smell. We have instinct and intuition. We are feeling beings with emotion. We are spirit imbued with the force of life—aware—and through our perception, dreamers.

For years, I had a very hard time understanding the Toltec perspective that we are always dreaming. I thought it meant nothing was real. That's not exactly true. What it means is that our awareness is alive and that we don't accurately experience what is in front of us, but perceive instead a virtual image distorted by a membrane of film filled with the activity of the dreaming mind. The image we see is not just a picture, but a living representation remade by the filter of our beliefs.

Our personal dream, our individual virtual reality, is the solid and familiar story we exist in. It becomes so familiar that we no longer even notice it. Only when something drastic happens to suspend or alter it—like an accident, illness, sudden loss, or other tragedy—do we get a glimpse of the world without our usual filter. In those moments, the mirage evaporates and we begin to see the limitless possibilities available by changing what we believe.

Years ago after a trip into the interior of Mexico, I came down with malaria. At first my doctor thought it was the flu. Once the diagnosis was made, my doctor was pretty excited (you don't see a lot of malaria in Colorado). I was very sick with a high fever. Six weeks later, I finally started to get better, but I was still weak and had lost a lot of weight.

Some friends of mine took me out for a walk in a local mountain park. They thought it would do me good to get outside into the fresh spring air. We walked for a short way and then I decided we should turn back because I was getting tired. Just as we turned around to go back, we passed a man and a woman walking the other way. The man called my name. He said, "Ray?" I turned around and looked at him. He seemed very pleasant but I didn't recognize him. I began to walk away. "Ray?" he said again. I looked harder. I had a warm feeling looking at him. His face was bathed in light and seemed very soft, like the effect you get when you spread gel on a camera lens. Still I couldn't recall his face and so I started to walk down the hill. He called out loudly, "Ray!" I looked back at him and struggled to place him. I stared directly at him for what seemed to me to be a very long time. All of a sudden, I heard a popping sound as if something that had been stuck released, and there was a return to a more familiar feeling.

I could now see this was Steve, a man I'd known for several years. Steve worked at the same company I did. I liked him and thought he was immensely intelligent, but we would often disagree because I thought he had a habit of rushing into things with way more enthusiasm than planning. Like just about everyone else in my life I had a judgment about him. My long illness, however, had severely diminished my attachment to just about everything—my possessions, my personal history, and my judgments. Much of what I had deemed serious and important was no longer even worth considering. I just didn't have the energy to maintain being right. Part of my world before I became sick was Steve; the way I interpreted him, defined him, and even gossiped about him. Because the illness had largely dissolved that, I saw him in a very different way. So different in fact I could not even recognize him.

Chapter 2

THE PATH TO NOW

> What you are experiencing in this very moment is the culmination of everything you have agreed to believe.

In order to change any of the beliefs that are holding you back from creating the life you want, you will need to understand how they were formed and what got you to this point.

For many years behavioral scientists have studied human infants to determine what their experience is and how they develop. Very small children can't express in words what is happening to them, so all we can do is observe. Just looking at a baby you can see that their eyes act like the lens of a video camera. Their attention shifts from moment to moment. They focus on whatever is enchanting, interesting, and catches their eye. They stare at it until it holds no more fascination and then move their attention to something else. They seem to gravitate towards what gives them pleasure and move away from what is confusing or doesn't feel good. What they perceive, what channels of communication they establish, and what they experience are determined solely by where they focus their attention.

Babies and toddlers are little human beings without language. They don't possess the ability to express to others in words what they are experiencing. They observe the world through the five physical senses and their intuitive sense of feeling. How things feel is a big part of how they perceive and process their surroundings. Unlike adults, who use words to describe what they feel, babies don't have language to interpret the emotion, yet their emotional awareness carries lots of information about the essence of what is happening moment to moment.

A woman I know was in the process of deciding whether she and her husband would get a divorce. They were still living together, but emotionally they had already separated. They had a two-year-old son who was walking but had not yet begun to speak. He would routinely make them sit down on the couch and insist they hold hands. Although he didn't have the ability to understand the words they were speaking, he could sense exactly what was going on between them. It didn't feel good, so he took action to make it different.

Little children exist in a kind of paradise. They have the capacity to perceive what is without a lot of distortion, unlike the adults who interpret everything through their agreements. Little children notice the essence of things guided by the truth of their emotions. Emotions never lie. They advise based on how it feels.

These little humans are free to be who they are. Sometimes they hurt and sometimes they are afraid, but they live in the present moment with a great capacity to enjoy life—to play, to be endlessly curious, and to love.

As adults, we need to be able to communicate with the little children. We want to give instructions, ask questions, and when necessary, take control. Adults have a basic understanding of their small children through a series of nonverbal clues, but have to establish a better channel of communication. In order to better communicate, children need to learn the code. They need to learn language. Once the code is understood, information can be given.

The passing of any information requires the focus of our awareness. The focus of our awareness is our attention. We receive pictures, sounds, feelings, and words from any situation through our attention. To learn anything we have to pay attention.

By capturing our attention and teaching us the code, the adults passed on to us their personal view of the world. They taught us how everything is. They told us their opinions about everybody and what they thought of themselves. They told us what we are and maybe more importantly what we are not. It's like downloading a program onto a computer. Unfortunately, if it is a view of the world infected with irrational fear, it acts like a virus in the program, creating agreements and eventually beliefs anchored in the very same fear.

One of my clients told me a story about his fear of heights. For as long as he could remember, he had been afraid of ledges, cliffs, and stairs to high places. In working toward his belief about this, he remembered that as a kid his mother had shrieked at him when he got too close to the edge of a pool, stood on a wall, or tried to climb a tree. "David!" she would yell. "Be careful! Look out!" His fear was her fear of heights, and she had infected him with it.

By catching our attention the adults create a channel of communication and inoculate us by way of the broadcast that comes through the channel. Through our attention there is a transmission with each person—a broadcast of his or her personal dream in that moment. It is way more than just words. Like a movie it has sound, color, movement, emotional tension, ambience, and texture. The channel of communication is like two movie projectors with images, thoughts, sounds, and meaning riding the light back and forth between the attention of the human beings.

Each concept the adults tell us about, each opinion they share is the way they reveal their personal dream. What they are sharing is their perception of the world altered by their own unique filter of belief. These lessons come in many different forms, but when our attention is hooked, when we focus our awareness, an impression is made. This process of capturing our attention for the first time creates our initial personal dream of how the world is. Seizing our attention for the first time is what the Toltecs called "The Dream of the First Attention" or what I will call *The First Dream.*

Over time and through repetition these impressions become alive in your mind, but only when you agree to whatever idea, point of view, or opinion is presented. All genuine communication is by agreement. For a solid channel of communication to be opened we have to agree on an interpretation of the raw data reaching us as light rays and sound waves. If you and I were to talk about cooking, for example, we would need to have a basic agreement about the function and name for things in a kitchen. Each of us modifies what we perceive creating our own individual virtual reality, so opening a complete channel of communication requires a similar interpretation, a shared distortion, if you will.

For little children acceptance of this distortion is not by choice but a requirement for survival. As a child, you had very little choice. Your name, the language you speak, where you lived, and where you went to school were all choices you had no say in. Maybe the adults even decided what you were supposed to believe, but in order for any of their opinions, points of view, or beliefs to begin to take hold, you had to agree.

To illustrate this, imagine a small boy playing in his parents' house. His mother has left him alone while she is working in another part of the house. He finds some big colorful markers and starts drawing on the wall. He's totally absorbed in what he is doing and having a great time. He has a big grin on his face. Drawing pictures on the wall is pure pleasure for him.

Suddenly his mother comes back into the room. She sees him, comes up behind him, and smacks him on the bottom, yelling, "I don't have time for this! You make me so mad! You're ruining my life! If it weren't for you I could have a life!" Her anger shakes him out of his dream. His attention is now hooked by her rage. His emotion is overwhelming, yet absolutely authentic. He is hurt because what just happened was *not-love*.

Suppose in his own way the little boy agrees with what she has said. Maybe he thinks, "She doesn't want me anymore because I'm ruining her life." As a reaction to the emotion he felt and his agreement, he makes a decision about what happened and that becomes his story. Maybe he decides being high-spirited and creative is not okay. Perhaps he decides he will run away and then she will be better off, or that he's responsible for her anger and if he wants her to love him again, he has to be different.

As the years go by the pattern continues. His mom is constantly overwhelmed, routinely reacting in frustration to what is normal when you have children around the house. He never knows what to expect. She slams doors, yells, and even breaks things when he doesn't act the way she wants him to. He feels trapped with nowhere to go. Each time it happens he feels a similar emotion and makes more and more decisions. *I won't do what you tell me to. If you don't like me, then I don't like you. I can't wait to get out of here.*

An agreement grows stronger through reinforcement and repetition. Incidents repeated over and over again in many different forms all carrying the same general message become very strong beliefs. Once they take hold, they have a life of their own. Although they start out as someone else's opinion, we agree and interpret things in our own way, making it our story. It becomes the story of our life. Not a story with a beginning, middle, and an end but the way we, the storyteller, describe everything and everyone in our life. It's a story based on what we have agreed to believe about everything that has happened to us.

Memories and the stories we make up to support our interpretation of what happened have an emotional point of view. However, the story corrupts what we remember. Now when something happens that is in any way similar to what is in our memory, the belief beneath it rises to the surface, appearing first as a vaguely familiar emotion.

Imagine the little boy is now a young man. He has a job and he tries his best to make a good impression.

He works hard and wants everyone to notice he is doing a good job.

One afternoon at work, his boss comes in suddenly and catches him joking around with some of his friends. She looks angry and tells them they need to get back to work or they are all going to be in trouble. She says something sarcastic and leaves quickly, slamming the door. The whole scene upsets him. There is an emotional surge that is somehow familiar. His mind starts racing. *It's not fair. We weren't doing anything wrong. Who does she think she is? I'll start looking for another job tomorrow.*

Something invisible and deep has been touched, and what appears first is the emotional point of view. His strategy to be accepted, the mask he shows everyone at work, is penetrated. The belief that he is not wanted and the memory of an unpredictable parent come alive and are now in control of his attention. The belief is expressing itself through his behavior, his emotion, and the conversation he is having with himself in his mind.

The adults who captured our attention for the first time, creating our initial personal dream of the world, were only passing on what they learned from the adults when they were children. The same thing happened to all of our friends, and so as children we are influenced not only by our own inner circle of adults, but by the circle of adults around our playmates and schoolmates as well.

This dynamic is neither good nor bad. It's how knowledge, traditions, and legacies are passed down from generation to generation. Sometimes, however, what gets transmitted hobbles us. As little children, we live in a world full of wonderment, possibility, and imagination. Because we have our integrity intact, we believe *I Am* and *I Can.* We believe things like: *I am wanted, I am beautiful, I am loved, I can do anything* . . . and so on. Often the grown-ups introduce an entirely different outlook. An outlook handed down from generation to generation based in fear.

The adults are stronger, bigger, and have the power. If we are assaulted by an outlook strangled with unreasonable fear, beyond good parenting and sound discipline, we may feel there is something terribly wrong. We rebel. We say "No!" Eventually those in charge wear us down. At some point we capitulate, overpowered and outmaneuvered. Our little village has been under siege for days, months, maybe even years. Defeated, we come out of the gates waving the white flag and declare, "I surrender. I give up. I agree." *I Can* becomes *I Can't. I Am* becomes *I'm Not.*

This is the path to now. What you are experiencing in this very moment is the culmination of everything you have agreed to believe. As the adults capture our attention and teach us the interpretation of perception—language—they open channels of communication into their own personal dream. We are slowly pulled from paradise. In the construction of The First Dream we go from operating with the intelligence of what we feel and develop a thinking mind filled with words. In our march towards physical maturity, we lose the ability to notice the essence of the present moment and become dominated by the intellect and reason. Over time each opinion, each idea, each concept makes an impression but only if we agree. If the adults in charge domesticate us under the boot of their fear, we will recycle many of their views into our beliefs even if we outwardly reject them. At a certain point we become overpowered by a runaway mind and frequent emotional reactions. At this juncture, our beliefs are in complete control of our attention. In The First Dream, our beliefs control our attention.

Of course, not every belief created on the path to now is limiting, nor is every limiting belief a barrier to achievement. In the fabrication of The First Dream many wonderful and positive things happen that support us in creating and living the life we love. Everyone has memories of joyful encounters, wise teachings, and gifts of compassion that helped them bloom. Identifying the core beliefs that enhance your life is important, yet to exact real and lasting change it is necessary to recognize any belief that is keeping you from realizing the happiness and success you want in life. By focusing your attention for a second time with awareness, you can create a whole new dream of life—an extraordinary life—this time carefully choosing what you want to believe.

Chapter 3

THE ISLAND OF THE KNOWN

Your personal Island of the Known is the result of what you've agreed to and where you have invested your faith. It is the container of "me" bounded by what you believe.

I magine the beginning of a movie. The camera starts with a panoramic view of the town. The view narrows to a particular part of town, down a street, and then finally to a specific house. In the scene, you are introduced to what is happening in front of the house. The eye of the camera goes into the house, up the stairs, and begins to pan around the room until it stops on the character that is of the most interest in the story. The main character. As you follow the viewpoint presented by the camera, you get introduced to the environment the main character lives in and to all the other characters in the story. You see what's happening around them, who is in their lives each day, what is working for them, and what they are struggling with. Through this window into their world, you begin to understand what's going on. Once you understand what's happening, you can relate to them and get involved in the story.

We each live in our own world just like the main character in the movie. Everyone we have ever met, everywhere we have ever lived, all the jobs we have ever had, all the trips we have been on, all the memorable events (good and bad)—everything that has ever happened to us constitutes our Island of the Known. Our own personal island constructed of our beliefs, other people's opinions, and all our knowledge, concepts, and experiences.

This island is bolstered by our description of everything. We assess and interpret what we experience moment to moment using all our knowledge to describe our personal view of the world to ourselves. This constant stream of words in our head is continually telling us what we know.

One of the reasons we do this is safety. The Island of the Known is really an island of safety. We need to explain things so they fit within the boundaries of the Island of the Known. If something is unexplainable then it exists outside the limits of the island and is unknown.

In the great Age of Discovery, the ancient mapmakers had a device for dealing with the limits of their knowledge: They drew an edge to the world and a boundless sea beyond. Some showed it filled with huge whirlpools and imaginary creatures while others just wrote, "Here there be dragons."

We are often afraid of what is beyond the boundary of what we know. If by chance we encounter it, we may dismiss it, make assumptions about it, pass judgment on it, or even pretend it doesn't exist. It takes courage to explore the unknown, expand our boundaries, and then encompass what we discover as known.

We normally assess what we see based on our Island of the Known. We focus in tightly and if what is before us has never been on our Island of the Known, we tend not to see it. There was a famous experiment by anthropologists in the 1920s with the Me'en people, a primitive tribe located in Ethiopia. Up to that point, they had no exposure to modern civilization. When photographs of people and animals were shown to them, they felt the paper, tasted it and sniffed it, yet they were unable to recognize the two-dimensional images in the pictures.

Even a giant leap of technology fueled by genius can be severely limited by what is on the Island of the Known. Alexander Graham Bell, inventor of the telephone, envisioned his creation as a way to deliver news and classical music to subscribers. Only after being presented with mounds of evidence, over a long period of time, could he be convinced that people were actually using his device to talk to each other.

What is on your Island of the Known is your truth, yet very often it is only true for you. Your personal Island of the Known is the result of what you've agreed to and where you have invested your faith. It is the container of "me" bounded by what you believe.

In the construction of The First Dream the adults captured our attention, taught us language, and opened channels of communication into their own personal dream by sharing their knowledge and opinions about everything. Much of what is on our Island of the Known is actually other people's opinions about how things are and how we are.

Most of us develop a lot of opinions because we are not okay not knowing. We like things explained and sewn up into a nice little package. We feel unsafe not knowing what will happen next. Who's going to do what. Who might say what. Who might act this way and who's going to act that way. In order to make something known we usually fill in the blanks and make a habit of assuming things. We put a lot of energy into creating something that makes us feel safe. We feel better saying, "That's how it is," or "This is what will happen," even if it isn't completely true.

In dealing with the unknown, people often turn to superstition. Superstition creates tremendous barriers to awareness because it superimposes explanations and assumptions that take a great deal of energy to hold together. They use props and invent answers steeped in superstition because of their inability to feel comfortable saying, "I just don't know."

With the fall of Roman civilization in the fifth century, Europe plunged into a Dark Age of superstition. In dealing with something as powerful and unpredictable as nature, humans at that time needed to impose a system that provided some sort of an answer to what they were seeing. In medieval Europe the order of the universe was explained as: The Earth is flat, if you venture out too far you'll fall off, and the Sun revolves around the Earth. What was true then is still true now—we see what we want to see according to what we believe.

Because of our insatiable need to know, we develop expectations. Expectation is an assumption about how something is supposed to happen. Unfortunately, expectation is often the mother of crisis. When something doesn't happen as expected, it can create a personal crisis.

An example: Let's say you are going to the airport to take a trip on an airplane. You have made the journey before. You know the way, about how long it takes to get there, and where to park. You are familiar with the routine once you get into the airport with tickets, security, and boarding. You have a pretty good idea what to expect. On the way into the airport, your car suddenly stops working and you have to pull over on the side of the road. You are going to miss your plane!

In a situation like missing a flight, most of us struggle with the uncertainty of what might happen next. We get distressed because things are not going as expected. In a crisis, when our expectations fail us, we are always off the Island of the Known.

The desire to put everything into the boundaries of the Island of the Known is very strong. This is why we tend to assume things. We need to know what will happen if we do this or if we do that. We second-guess. We predict. We assume our perception is the extent of possibility and that others see things the way we do. Because of past history we assume we know what people will do, how they will react, and what they will probably say.

When we meet someone for the first time we ask, "What do you do for a living?" We guess their age, look at their clothes, and listen to how they talk. If we can't collect enough information we tend to assume a lot about them. We need to define the people we don't know and put them into the boundaries of what we do know. We need to create an assessment, an interpretation, so they become known. Only then can we form an opinion and a description that makes sense.

Years ago I was traveling with a couple in Italy, and we went to a reservation center on the outskirts of Venice. This center booked rooms for many of the hotels inside the town. We were looking for some moderately priced rooms and had the reservation person call a hotel to see if they had a vacancy. The hotel clerk put the reservation person on hold. Immediately my traveling companions started to talk nervously about what we would do if a moderately priced room was not available. Maybe we would need to book an expensive four-star hotel room! There was a lot of heated discussion around it. As soon as the hotel put the reservation clerk on hold, the couple went into the unknown. They had no idea what would happen next. They were unable to wait and see what might happen. They had to make a plan. Discuss. Argue. Project an outcome by assuming things. That way they felt better because they were back on their Island of the Known.

The need to keep everything on the Island of the Known is very powerful. Have you ever been traveling, woken up in a strange place, and for just a moment not known where you were? It can be very unsettling. Nothing makes sense. We don't feel right until a window is a window and we know what is behind every door. We need to make everything solid. Rock solid.

As the structure of the Island of the Known begins to take form, we demand clarity. We need to know, but as we seek more and more information the knowledge begins to rule us. All that information is constantly telling us what is going on right in front of our eyes. The runaway chatter of the mind has our attention almost all the time. Knowledge, expressing itself through the voice in our head, becomes like God—all knowing and all seeing.

Our whole story—the boundaries of the Island of the Known—keeps us safe. Safe from whatever we are afraid of. Even if we are miserable it explains everything. We know who we are, and what we can and cannot do. We make up a story about how everything is, and become so invested in our story we will defend it at any cost. We collect evidence so we can easily justify our stories. Why this is possible and that is impossible. Why I get along with him and why I can't get along with her. Why this will work and that will never work. Why things always end up this way. We describe ourselves with stories. "I have a temper." "I'm not a morning person." "I've always been this way." It's familiar. We have a lot of attachment to our story on the Island of the Known. It's our image and identity. It's "me." It's "my life." It's "who I am." We make up some sort of story so everything fits in its box, carefully laid next to all the boxes on the Island of the Known.

It takes a lot of energy to hold together your Island of the Known. When I was in grade school, I remember playing with my friends in the woods near the school and coming upon the remains of an old asphalt road. The plants growing underneath it and over it had cracked it, buckled it, and heaved it over the years. The forest and the freezing and thawing of the earth had reclaimed it back to nature. As long as the road, a man-made structure, had received attention through maintenance, the road had remained a road. When the energy of human attention was with-drawn, the natural forces took over and the road dis-integrated. Its existence was dependent on continual patching, constantly reinforcing the structure.

Our whole framework, our Island of the Known, is very similar to that. It is based on what we believe—what we have invested our faith in. We pour lots of energy into it, maintaining it and grooming it. The run-away voice in our mind that worries, schemes, frets, plans, discusses, and argues works day and night forti-fying the road of what we know.

We tend the road each day with total dedication, taking complete responsibility for its care. There is a moment when we are just waking up, riding an edge between two worlds—the asleep world and the every-day awake world. As soon as we are fully awake, we begin to remember who we are, what we are, and where we are. Our familiar dialog kicks in and off we go! All at once, we are deeply immersed in our current description of the world. Every morning we awaken from our nightly sleep and start the motor of the mind, resurrecting our personal Island of the Known.

We invest lots of energy assuming things and keeping up descriptions that may or may not be true. The obsession to interpret and define everything severely constrains our ability to perceive what is really happening. On the Island of the Known, we limit our nearly limitless possibilities. In the endless pursuit of information so we can control our world and feel safe, we become what we study and the information now controls us. The Island of the Known is a container of our own making and like water, we take the form of the container.

What would happen if you suddenly stepped off your Island of the Known? What would happen if you stopped your interpretation of everything, even for just one moment, allowing yourself to observe the world without your habitual lens of belief? What you might see is a new world of possibility without the story. Your story.

In the movie *The Truman Show,* the main character grows up in a made-up world that is actually a television stage. In the film, his life has been broadcast as a TV show every day since he was born. He is now grown up, married, and lives on a fake island in a town full of actors. He has no knowledge of this and believes he is living a normal life until a series of technical flaws begins to dispel the illusion. He starts to question what is authentic. Towards the end of the movie, he is in complete conflict with what he once accepted as true and tries to escape by taking a sailboat out onto the ocean. Instead of finding a way out, he runs into a theatrical backdrop painted to look like the horizon on the ocean. At first he is confused, but as his disbelief of what he is witnessing begins to evaporate, he clearly sees the construct of his world. He finds a door in the backdrop, opens it, and for the first time in his life sees the world that lies beyond the boundary of the enormous television stage. In that moment he steps off his Island of the Known to a new and yet unknown freedom.

We generally accept the reality of the world with which we are presented. We become fashioned by the culture we live in and by the language we speak. We think we are what we think. We live on our own personal mesa bounded by our beliefs, concepts, agreements, and other people's opinions.

If you really want to change what you believe, venture off your Island of the Known. By stepping off this island you may discover a whole other world. A world of mind-altering possibility.

Stepping off the Island of the Known requires two things. The first one is awareness. Awareness of what is on your Island of the Known. This first step is about clearly seeing the boundaries created by what you believe about yourself and everything around you. Pay attention to what you keep saying to yourself about yourself. When you speak about yourself to others, what do you say? How do you introduce yourself? What do you keep saying about other people, money, work, or love? Become aware of what's in your life that you identify with, what you defend, what you are attached to, and what really scares you when you consider giving it up.

The second requirement for stepping off the Island of the Known is letting go of always needing to know—always needing to know *why*. Do you have a habit of assuming things? When unexpected things happen, how do you respond? Try, even for just a moment, giving up your expectations about how everything is *supposed* to be. Can you really be sure how people will act or in what direction things might go? Can you be absolutely certain what might happen next? Experiment with letting go of the addiction to filling in the blanks and allow your experience to unfold in front of you.

The Island of the Known is often constructed for survival. Letting go of tight-fisted control can be a scary thing. All of a sudden the ground beneath your feet isn't as solid as you thought it was. To see life as it is, you have to step away from your concept of what it is or you just won't see it. To begin, venture off the Island of the Known.

Chapter 4

FAITH AND THE BROKEN HEART

The grinding to dust of the old structure is a gift, not an excuse to suffer. Recognizing the beliefs born of the broken heart and changing the decisions made so long ago begin a new journey, releasing your passion and true power.

As time passes we adopt the lessons of The First Dream and build our own life. What was once other people's construction of reality becomes our own unique structure. We redecorate—painting it the colors we like, buying curtains and putting in new carpet. From the dream that is passed on to us from the adults, we develop our own opinions and points of view. We continually re-form and strengthen our personal Island of the Known until it defines the boundaries of "me."

The fabrication of the Island of the Known creates a structure that gives us a recognizable form and a solid identity. We assemble information and create many stories about who we are and what the world is, fortifying the framework.

Maybe we have an underlying anxiety about things, but the structure of the Island of the Known is designed to help us interpret what is happening in our life so we can feel relatively safe. As long as almost everything can be explained and then assimilated within the borders of the Island of the Known, we do feel safe. It really doesn't matter if some of these ideas make us happy or sad. It doesn't matter if some of these things work well for us and others do not. The habit of assessing everything through our filter of belief makes the world outside familiar and therefore known.

Unavoidably and without exception certain parts of our personal construction, the Island of the Known, fall apart. One example is when a romantic relationship unravels. Imagine that you walk into a restaurant and unexpectedly see the person you love passionately kissing someone else. It's as if the floor beneath you begins to tilt. You become disoriented and it's very hard to focus. A piece of what is known has been detonated. It's like getting the breath knocked out of you. You are devastated and it hurts, usually right around the area of the heart. It feels as if your heart has been broken.

Having your heart broken can happen in so many ways. Losing a job. You or someone close to you gets injured or becomes very ill. Someone you know well dies. The breakup of a romantic relationship. Divorce. You are betrayed and lose trust in something or someone. For kids it might be a trip they were looking forward to that never happens, failing a test, a best friend who moves away, an adult who breaks a sacred agreement, or a parent who doesn't understand them and lets them down repeatedly.

Being heartbroken begins as a shock and quickly moves into grief, sometimes with intense emotional pain. The pain of grief is largely about our resistance to the unraveling of what is familiar. Our attachment to how things are *supposed to be* causes great suffering when things fall apart. In effect, the structure we have built collapses. Eventually we adapt—we have to. Somehow we need to function, and we must stop the pain and confusion in order to get back on track. We rebuild with one singular purpose—to stop the suffering. We never, ever want to hurt that way again.

What is interesting is that the emotion that occurs in the moment of the heartbreak is authentic and doesn't lie. Emotions never lie. What you feel is telling you the truth and the truth is always good information. But we don't leave it at that. We react, concocting an agreement with ourselves about what happened and then create a story about it that justifies the agreement.

When everything falls apart, we naturally encounter grief. There are five stages in the process of grief. Denial, anger, bargaining, depression, and the last stage—acceptance. Since we are heartbroken, the last stage never becomes complete. It gets bypassed and we form a new relationship with reality, building a bigger fortress. We manufacture protection. We develop masks to hide behind and find things to act as crutches to help us walk around without so much pain.

Once the island is fortified, we think we are safe but we're not. Whatever it is we devise to protect ourselves sets us up for the next heartbreak. If our personal construction is built to make us safe from the old heartbreak, then it is built on a foundation of sand. What we are so afraid of inevitably happens again. And again. And again. So we rebuild. Each time with a more rigid system of protection than before. But time passes and we forget. What we have created to protect us rolls in like a fog when there is any danger of getting hurt that way again. We don't see that the most recent emotional crisis is part of a string of heartbreaks started so long ago.

The First Heartbreak comes when we are children. Small children have an unspoken agreement with their parents. *I can be myself, and you will love me unconditionally. You will protect me, and I'm safe with you. I can trust you, and you will take care of me. I can count on you to be there for me.* Invariably that agreement is broken many times. When a child's world collapses it hurts terribly, so they devise some sort of strategy to adapt. They invent a method to survive.

One of my coaching clients, Mike, loved to play baseball as a child. His father owned several car dealerships and hardly had any time for Mike. He frequently criticized Mike and was hard to please. Mike was good at baseball and wanted his father to see his performance on the field. Then he'd be pleased! However, his father almost never came to his games. At first, Mike would watch with nervousness, his attention half on the game and half on the parking lot. This went on game after game. The next year during baseball season Mike got angry about it. "He's never coming. Forget it. He doesn't care." In later years when his father did come to a game, it actually made him nervous that he had shown up. "Why is he here? What does *he* want?" Mike was angry and developed aloofness and arrogance as a reaction to his father's hardly ever attending his games. It was his strategy not to get hurt that way ever again. Over the years he practiced and perfected it. As an adult, it became a masterful art he used in business and in his personal relationships. His aloofness, arrogance, and anger became his armor, shield, and sword.

The strategies against being heartbroken are designed to protect us from being hurt in the same way again. One way to do this is to wear a mask. The mask helps us pretend to be someone we are not because we're afraid we will be rejected if we are seen as we are. We develop masks for our parents, for our job, for our friends, and for our lovers because we learned long ago it is not safe to be exposed. We can be arrogant, or we can become invisible. We can smile all the time, being the friendliest person in the world, or we can be harsh with everyone. We may make others wrong to substantiate our position or find flaws with everyone to justify keeping our distance. We might practice selfishness, act like a victim, or not trust anyone. We pretend in front of the mask so we can hide behind the mask.

The fallout from being brokenhearted is that we make up all sorts of stories that prevent us from really living. The passion in living is about taking the risk to connect with life! Living with all that protection dissolves our courage and strangles our passion. When we lose our passion, we find ourselves allowing things to choose us because it is safer than doing the choosing. Revealing our passion becomes too dangerous because we risk what we have invested so much time and energy trying to protect.

The fortress built over time from all the heartbreak is held together with faith. Faith is the glue that binds all the individual beliefs together into the form of *me*—with all its rules and regulations, with all its opinions and points of view. Whenever a portion of our personal world collapses, we develop strategies to protect ourselves. Over the years we cover this ground again and again. We make it stronger each time we use it, and we continually modify the protection to suit the situation. We become wrapped up in what we believe because of our attachment to it. We identify with it. We look for evidence to support it and defend it at every turn. We become the masks we show everyone else. Eventually there is no awareness about what we are doing; it is just an unconscious emotional response triggered when what started as a simple heartbreak is in danger of happening all over again. It is like a spell we are under, an uncontrollable dream that arises and lives our life for us. Over time, the decisions we make when things fall apart become a vault housing a large portion of our faith.

What is really true for you—what is automatic and compelling—is where you have placed your faith. One of the most powerful things influencing any behavior holding you back is where you have invested your faith, especially in agreements arising from the broken heart. Becoming aware of those agreements and reshaping them can create extraordinary changes in the way you meet life every day.

Becoming aware of the beliefs born when you were heartbroken provides an immense opportunity to shift your faith. See if you can remember when you had your heart broken from different periods in your life. Go back to each moment. Allow the memory to inform you and notice how you feel. What did you decide about what happened to you? What stopped the pain? What have you created over time that has made you safe? When you do those things now, how does it feel?

There is a fork in the road when you encounter the broken heart. There is real opportunity down one path and a narrowing of life itself down the other. When you choose protection, you learn how to shut down, hold back your passion, and hide your love. With awareness, the opportunity exists—*right now*—to expand and step off the Island of the Known. The grinding to dust of the old structure is a gift, not an excuse to suffer. Recognizing the beliefs born from a broken heart and changing the decisions made so long ago begin a new journey, releasing your passion and true power.

Part II

The Second Dream

Chapter 5

THE FIRST STEP: PRACTICE AWARENESS

The posture of awareness is not caught up in the action, but rather observes the action. It's a stance that teaches impeccable perception by watching, feeling, and listening without the interpreter always explaining what you are seeing right in front of your eyes.

There are four simple steps required to change a belief. The first and most important step is practicing awareness. The mind is alive, naturally aware, and always dreaming, but we become so distracted by the conversation in our head dominating our attention we lose the ability to notice. We lose the ability to notice what has been created by what we believe. We even stop noticing the beliefs themselves. To transform any belief takes awareness. Awareness of what you really believe. In the process of changing a belief, if you can recover your awareness you're almost there. Developing a habit of awareness is most of the task—perhaps 90 percent of the journey. In order to recover your awareness, you must practice awareness.

Recovering your awareness allows you to separate yourself from your habitual point of view so you can observe your point of view. Practicing awareness permits you to become the witness to your own reactions and the stories that emerge from those reactions. This is no easy task. You have a sense of "me" and your image is invested there. All the memories, experiences, stories, agreements, and beliefs that populate the Island of the Known have become the dominant dreamer of your life, interpreting everything that comes into view.

This *Interpreter* has a distinct point of view and it's always telling you how everything is. It uses all your knowledge and experience as a library to find evidence to support its description of the world. The interpreter is not a perceiver because thinking is not a tool of perception. Thinking is a tool of analysis. The interpreter is the gatekeeper of perception and the stronger it is, the less awareness you actually have of what is really going on.

It is not possible to practice awareness by allowing the Interpreter to describe and define everything you notice. Using the vantage point of the interpreter to examine itself is much like having criminals guard the prison. The interpreter born of The First Dream cannot observe itself with any accuracy because it distorts everything according to its filter of belief.

Practicing awareness requires a whole different approach. Do you remember the book *A Christmas Carol* by Charles Dickens? The main character, Ebenezer Scrooge, is visited on Christmas Eve by three ghosts: the ghost of Christmas past, the ghost of Christmas present, and the ghost of Christmas to come. Over the course of the evening, each ghost takes Scrooge to view himself in a scene from his life. It is as if he is watching himself in a play. The story of *A Christmas Carol* illustrates the perspective of having true awareness of yourself. In the story, Ebenezer Scrooge becomes the observer of his life by standing outside the boundaries of his Island of the Known.

Achieving the perspective of awareness of yourself is only possible by becoming the observer of your life. An observer with a specific purpose—hunting. What you are hunting is the expression of beliefs that are not serving you. What you are hunting is limiting beliefs based in fear that are obstacles keeping you from being as happy and successful as you want to be. When practicing awareness, the observer is the *Hunter of Beliefs.*

Belief is the prey you are hunting. In order to hunt prey you need to know something about it. It helps to understand its behavior, its habits, and its patterns. Belief is way more than an idea. Belief is alive, a distinct point of view expressing itself through your behavior, in how you feel and in what you say. In order to be effective, the Hunter of Beliefs needs to learn all about its prey and so is always vigilant, tracking the expression of those beliefs.

There is a posture or attitude required to effectively hunt belief. It is very similar to the way the big cats—lions, tigers, jaguars, and cheetahs—hunt. They are intent, intense, and focused. They are acutely aware, always looking for movement. They're not lost in thinking but rather watch with all their senses engaged. Big cats can remain at rest for long periods of time, yet they are ready to explode into action at the sight of prey. They aren't concerned how it happens. If the prey goes left when they expected it to go right, they are not personally offended. They are masters of awareness, possessing a certain wisdom— what the Native Americans called animal wisdom. This wisdom is a very useful tool for understanding and practicing awareness.

I have a visualization exercise I give my students and clients where they imagine they are a tiger hunting in the jungle. They dream, while awake, that they are perceiving the jungle from this unusual perspective. Slowly and deliberately, they acclimate to the attributes of the tiger: standing on all fours, being covered in fur, having a tail, listening with ears erect, and panting with their mouth slightly open through very large teeth. Rather than approaching the idea of being a hunter as intellectual knowledge, they develop an inner knowing words cannot express. Through active imagination they get an experience of what being the tiger *feels* like.

The posture of the cat is the posture of awareness. The posture of awareness is not caught up in the action, but rather observes the action. It's a stance that teaches impeccable perception by watching, feeling, and listening without the Interpreter explaining what you are seeing right in front of your eyes.

Getting the Interpreter to quiet down is a critical step in recovering your awareness. In the martial arts, as in many of the spiritual traditions from around the world, one of the first tasks given to any new student is to learn to stop the chatter of the mind. This practice has many names. Mindfulness. Meditation. Reflection. The Toltecs had a method of ceasing the internal dialog they called "stopping the world."[1] Learning to stop the world gives you the opportunity to see what's going on without the fog of the Interpreter analyzing everything from the perspective of The First Dream.

Learning to stop the world builds the *will*. Will is the ability to deliberately decide, with unwavering intensity, on a course of action. Strengthening the will allows us to direct our attention, produce conscious focused thinking as well as stop the world.

The trick is to focus your attention on something as a ruse to quiet the mind. Holding that intention

---

[1]There is an exercise for quieting the mind called S*top the World* in part 3, "Tools."

and not letting it go to fidget or think about what's for dinner exercises the will. By stopping the dialog you reclaim some of the energy you normally invest in keeping your personal description of the world together. Learning to be still fosters awareness and is a sure step to venturing off the Island of the Known.

One obstacle to learning mindfulness is accepting the concept that all chatter in the mind is bad, must be stopped, and if you can't stop it there is something wrong with you. The mind is always dreaming; alive with pictures, reverie, imagination, inspiration, monologue, and dialog. Trying to hold back the dreaming mind during every waking moment would be like doing push-ups all day.

What creates drama for us are the wounds in the dreaming mind that fuel fear-based beliefs expressed by the Interpreter. To recognize, change, and heal these wounds requires awareness. By stopping the world and recovering our will, we begin to recover our awareness. Only then can we have any hope of becoming the Hunter of Beliefs, noticing our emotional reactions as they happen rather than unconsciously allowing them to dominate our attention.

When we are triggered by an event, our emotions take over because each part of the belief system has an emotional point of view. We awaken the giant and the belief casts a spell over us. We become overwhelmed by the emotion, and the perspective of the belief distorts everything we see. The emotion ignites a story and our story supports our interpretation of the emotion. Most of the time we're lucky if we even notice it, let alone know where it comes from or what the agreement really is.

An example: Let's say you are in a meeting at work and you have an idea about how to get something done. You notice just the thought of speaking about your idea leaves you feeling anxious. When it's your turn to talk and everyone is looking at you, the anxiety gets more intense. In the eye of the Hunter of Beliefs, there is the prey. That rise of anxiety signals the presence of what you are hunting.

When you have moments like that in your life, begin to notice. What are you telling yourself? How does your body feel? Has your expression changed? What is the quality of your breathing? How does everyone in the room look to you?

In the meeting, as the anxiety takes over, we may amp up our response. We might blurt out our idea hoping we don't get shot down. Our communication style might become defensive. Maybe the tone of our voice becomes softer and our delivery almost apologetic. These kinds of automatic, unconscious behaviors and the underlying emotion can reveal a lot about what we believe.

Hunting prey is about taking the time to stop and notice what is happening inside of your personal dream by using your will to focus your attention. By deliberately focusing your attention, you are practicing awareness. Without awareness, you are not the dreamer of your life but rather the one being dreamed.

When we have moments of emotional reaction things can become unreal almost as if we are navigating through a dream. As the Hunter of Beliefs, the opportunity in those moments is to notice the quality and texture of the dream.

Modern research on dreaming suggests that asleep dreams are not just messages but models of our inner world. While awake, our reason, physical body, and everything around us constitute the frame. During asleep dreaming our body and reason are paralyzed, the solid frame of the world is gone, so our brain builds a model entirely based on memories, experiences, beliefs, and agreements. The essence of this secondary world is very difficult to identify while we are awake in the solid world. One way to understand more of the workings of our inner world is lucid dreaming—having awareness and volition in the asleep dream.

Many ancient cultures practiced the art of lucid dreaming—becoming aware in the asleep dream. For more than 1,000 years Tibetan Buddhists have been practicing lucid dreaming as a means to approach enlightenment. Tibetan Dream Yoga is designed to incorporate a lifetime of spiritual practice into the moment of transition at death. The practice reminds the dying person (or the person meditating) to constantly recognize that all perception is merely the projection of one's own mind.

The aborigines of Australia describe the origins and culture of the land and its people as the Dream Time. The Dream Time contains many parts: It is the story of things that have happened, how the universe came to be, how human beings were created, and how the Creator intended humans to function within the cosmos. To them, only extraordinary states of consciousness through the practice of lucid dreaming can help one be aware of the inner dreaming of the Earth and the beings that live there.

The Toltecs also had a lucid dreaming practice. The idea was to remember while you were asleep that you were dreaming. To do this they would practice looking at their hands while awake and say to themselves, "Am I dreaming?" Eventually they hoped to remember to look at their hands in the asleep dream, triggering the thought, "Am I dreaming?" If you became aware you were dreaming, you could make choices in the dream. You now had the ability to notice what was going on. You could decide where to go, who to talk to, and what to do as long as you didn't wake up the Interpreter. If you were being chased in a recurring nightmare you could turn to your pursuer and say, "Who are you? What do you want?" Just that one lucid action could completely transform the dream.

The practice of lucid dreaming makes navigating at will while asleep dreaming possible, but the real benefit is to awaken and recover your awareness in the waking dream. The real point of lucid dreaming is to develop the art of *Lucid Living.*

Lucid Living is about recovering enough awareness to notice that the simulation you see in your brain is constantly being altered by your beliefs and agreements. To notice what you see is really there but filtered, interpreted, and modified by what you believe.

The mind is alive and we are dreaming all the time, day and night. To become aware of how your beliefs distort your perception, especially in moments of stress and emotional reaction, remember to look at your hands and say to yourself; "Wait a minute . . . hold on now. . . . What am I dreaming?"

Ask yourself questions about what you are noticing. *What just happened here? How do I feel? What am I telling myself? Is what I'm saying to myself absolutely true?* These are the *Questions of Disbelief.* Just remembering to ask these questions is a powerful turn of events that allows you to recover your awareness and see past the boundaries of your Island of the Known. The Questions of Disbelief break the spell of being completely convinced that you are the Interpreter and nothing more.

The practice of Lucid Living and remembering the Questions of Disbelief demands that you become skeptical and stop accepting everything you think as absolutely true. It requires that you don't completely trust all the things you say or what anyone else says, for that matter.

Remembering the Questions of Disbelief and attempting to practice Lucid Living reveal a war. A war for your attention. After years and years of habit, your attention has been captivated by the voice of your thinking. Listen to it and notice what it's saying. Really listen to it. If you listen closely it is telling you what you know. Reinforcing it. Discussing it like a lawyer argues a case. The advocate for what you believe. It discusses things like what happened that shouldn't have happened. What you should have done or what they should have done. What you need to do. Why you are right and they are wrong, or why they are right and you are wrong. These points of view are echoed by many voices. The *Voices of the First Dream*.

The Voices of the First Dream are outlets for the fearful parts of your belief system. It's much like a play. If you had something to say, a commentary about life, you would need a story and characters to express your viewpoint. The continual conversation in your mind, your behavior, and the stories you tell yourself about what happens to you are no different. They all serve to express what you really believe. Since you are hunting beliefs that keep you from being happy and effective, awareness of the expression of those beliefs can be very powerful in helping you make the changes you want in your life.

The Voices of the First Dream are easily recognized. There can be thousands of variations to a few well-defined archetypes, yet their expression is actually very simple. The part of the mind that harbors our wounds is tricky. It thrives on complexity and confusion, yet beliefs based in fear have a common root. Clearing away all that confusion reveals one core belief expressing itself in thousands of ways. *I Can't,* and *I'm Not.*

I'm not good enough. I'm not smart enough. I'm not wanted. I'm not okay as I am. I can't do it right. I can't get what I want . . . and on and on.

I Can't and *I'm Not* can also be projected onto other people. For example, if we expect someone to act in a certain way and they don't meet our expectation, how we react may sound a lot like, "You can't" and "You're not."

The loudest voices of the First Dream are *the Judge* and *the Victim.* The Judge always comments on how it *should* be. The Judge says things like, "You're doing it wrong. They're doing it wrong. You should be ashamed. They should be punished. They should act like this. You should act like that." Maybe your Judge is a cagey old man with a long white beard. Perhaps your Judge is the hanging judge from the old American West or is in a white wig scowling behind long black robes. The Judge is the critic and argues from all the rules about what is right and what is wrong. Your rules. Your *Book of Rules.*

The Judge is the voice of the *Demon of Perfection.* The Demon of Perfection says no matter what we do, no matter what we achieve, no matter how good it gets, it will *never* be good enough. This applies to us and is projected to everyone whose image appears in our virtual reality.

Every coin has two sides. On one side of the coin is the Judge and on the other side is the Victim. The Victim receives the judgment and agrees with the opinions of the Judge. The Victim says things like, "It's not my fault. No one ever listens to me. It's not fair. I can't help it. No matter what I do, it's never good enough." Maybe your Victim is the parent whose children never listened and hardly ever come to visit. Perhaps your Victim is someone whose past has ruined their future or who is mortally wounded by romantic love. The Victim complains and makes up "poor me" stories because the Victim has no gratitude. Gratitude is a state of being, thankful for all the gifts life offers in the present moment. The Victim is never in the present moment. The Victim looks to the past and believes everything would have been all right if *only*. . . . The Victim looks into the future and believes everything will be all right *when*. . . . It could be all right but in the mind of the Victim, it never will be.

Another voice of the First Dream is Belle, the saloon girl. The Prostitute. She wants to please everyone and can be anything you need her to be. She's the pretender. This is the voice that will compromise anything to get what we want. What we want is the prize. What we really want is the prize of love and acceptance. Her actions reveal an agreement that says, *I'll do whatever it takes just as long as everyone is happy—no matter how I feel.*

Take an inventory. How often do you do something because you think you should or because you feel obligated to? How often do you say yes with your mouth when the rest of you is saying no? What things in your life are you tolerating? Are you tolerating them out of fear, or out of love?

Suppose you are in a relationship and your partner wants to do something you would rather not do. To please them you go along. You say yes, but you're bored and resentful. You wear a smiling mask, but there is something churning underneath. In Spanish the word "mascara" means mask. Belle always wears lots of makeup. Lots of mascara. The mask hides why you say yes when you really mean no. The mask conceals the parts of you that you think no one else will accept. The mask hides the truth of how you feel.

Again, every coin has two sides. There is a much more respectable side of Belle. The white knight on the regal horse. The nurse mopping the brow of the wounded. The Rescuer. The Champion. The Hero. They say things like, "Don't worry about me, I'll be all right. I'll fix that for you. Let me do it. I can help you." Because they are two sides of the same coin, the belief of the hero, the champion and the rescuer is exactly the same as Belle's. *You are more important than I am, and if I do this I'll get what I want. If I act this way I'll get the prize.*

The Rescuer—the Champion—the Hero is a voice that reveals *I Can't* and *I'm Not* is a belief that has no respect. The actions of the Rescuer speak loudly saying, *I don't respect you enough to believe you can do it. That's because I don't believe I can do it either.*

There are many more Voices of the First Dream. They can act defiant, arrogant, aloof, obnoxious, selfish, needy, revengeful, or special—all expressing the same core belief. These are the voices of *I'm Not.* They open certain channels to express themselves using things like gossip, cursing, comparison, guilt, justification, defending, complaining, sarcasm, accusation, and lying.

Many beliefs expressed by the Voices of the First Dream have their roots in other people's opinions. Out of habit we analyze what we experience with the information we have gathered. Our knowledge largely consists of what we've learned over time—what we've read, heard, and seen. A lot of the input that makes up our library of knowledge is actually just other people's opinions. Imagine that. Perhaps 50 percent of the dialog chugging along in your mind is made up of other people's opinions!

Opinions are a powerful influence when they find a fertile mind. Let's say you are moving into a new neighborhood and the man next door comes over to welcome you. As he is introducing himself, he tells you that the woman across the street is very mean. The first time you see her you will probably wonder, "Is she really mean?" The seed has been planted.

The actions people take are the result of their opinions. If that action has a big effect on us, then the opinion can be contagious—but only if we have a similar distortion of perception. An example: It is well documented that violent incidents in the workplace or in schools are soon followed by copycat actions. Even something as drastic as school or workplace violence is merely an opinion that the action is a reasonable solution to a problem.

In addition to opinions we use concepts to support what we believe in an attempt to create a world that makes sense to us. Think about positive concepts— things like goodness, charity, love, service, responsibility, fidelity, honesty, hope, trust, generosity, kindness, wisdom, friendship, and integrity. Do you use these concepts as channels for wisdom as well as tools for creating an exceptional life, or do you use them as weapons to make yourself or other people wrong? Take the concept of responsibility, for example. If you close your eyes and put the word in front of you, you may get a sense of the meaning beyond what is written in the dictionary. There is something about the word that can actually help you feel connected to everyone. The word can act as a form directing your action as an expression of love. It is also easy to use this word as evidence of how you or others *should* act. You can use this concept as a way to make yourself right and other people wrong. The hanging Judge can make a pretty good argument about who is being responsible and who is not.

Another way to gain awareness about the beliefs of The First Dream is by watching the coauthors of that dream, the important adults in your life when you were a child. For most of us this was our parents. In The First Dream our parents were merely transferring their worldview to us. They inoculated us with their opinions, reacting to what was outside of them based on their own beliefs.

When we become adults we tend to have a whole list of judgments about our parents and respond to them according to those judgments. We create a series of agreements throughout the relationship, and we experience them through the lens of those agreements.

Consider taking another point of view. If either of your parents is still alive, the next time you are with them, try to see how they process the world. Watch how they react to what comes into their attention. Be the impartial scientific observer watching their behavior and hearing what they say with *no judgment.* What do you notice that seems familiar about their behavior? Is it something you do too?

Taking another point of view and developing awareness takes patience, persistence, and perseverance. Recovering your awareness is a process. Just when you think you've got it, another layer reveals itself. There always seems to be more to discover and even more after that.

Unfortunately, most of us want it fixed right now.

There is always a rush to solve the problem. If we want to change a belief, the drive is to get to the final step—creating a new agreement. To jump to the last step is a mistake, however. The importance of practicing awareness cannot be underestimated.

Normally we solve problems by thinking them through. We use our logic and gather all the information we need from the Island of the Known to come up with a solution. In the quest to change a belief, using this method is bound to fail. That's because belief is a living dream and so understanding it comes from more than just thinking about it. Awareness of it comes from hunting the dream and tracking its expression and influence in your life. Discernment comes from becoming the Hunter of Beliefs, Lucid Living, and asking the Questions of Disbelief. These actions alone will break the spell woven by the belief and start to put you back in the driver's seat.

Once we really understand the agreements we have made with ourselves—honestly, nakedly, and without lies—then and only then can we have any hope of changing them. But becoming aware of what we have agreed to and what that has created can be startling. Many of the beliefs we have are deep and pervasive, and their influence seems to be everywhere. At first it appears to be so complicated we think we'll never get to the bottom of it. There are so many twists and turns. But as we look closer, what seems to be many beliefs can stem from one single influence. If it is a limiting belief or a powerful agreement that creates emotional drama and holds us back, most likely it is our particular brand of *I'm Not.*

When we begin to have real awareness about an agreement we've made, we get a sense of how prevalent it is in our life. It's like when a rock hits the windshield of a car. At first there is a mark where it impacted the glass, but over time cracks spread out like a spider web across the windshield. We discover that for years we have been supporting and investing ourselves in the belief, and now we get caught in the web no matter where we move. The belief has become our all-purpose filter affecting everything: our work, our attitudes about money, our relationships—our life! All this awareness can become so overwhelming we get to the point where we just can't take anymore. We announce, *Enough! I've had it! I declare independence! I'm starting a revolution!*

Reclaiming your independence is an important step toward recovering your awareness. After becoming conscious of what has been created, it takes an enormous amount of will and a sharp intent to pick yourself up and move forward. Becoming truly fed up with an old belief that is holding you back is a virtue. The virtue of intolerance.

Create an inventory of your beliefs, especially ones you recognize as being fearful. Observe, in the best way you can, what you have come to believe, with absolute honesty. Notice when you tell stories about yourself if what you say sounds like the Victim or the Judge. Remember to ask the Questions of Disbelief. Observe if what you say and think is truly yours or just other people's opinions. These are the first steps to unraveling the enchantment you have been under, breaking the stranglehold of faith, and softening the boundaries of the Island of the Known.

Awareness of what you believe opens up a whole universe of possibility. If a limiting belief is based on someone else's opinion, a lie or something that is no longer true, and you see that with absolute certainty—the battle is almost over. It is the end of the domination of The First Dream and the start of a new beginning. A new beginning of building beliefs that support a life you can love.

Chapter 6

THE SECOND STEP:
GIVE UP THE NEED TO BE RIGHT

> Giving up the need to be right stops every avenue where the belief is expressing itself. It suspends justification and evidence gathering, blocking the primary source of nourishment—you.

The second step to changing a belief is letting it go. Releasing it. Freeing yourself from a belief, however, is far more than just an intellectual decision. Liberating yourself from a belief is often not as simple as deciding to disagree. Disengaging from a belief is more than a conclusion that you come to; it's an event with life-changing implications. Letting go of a belief is an act of will requiring that you take a precious jewel of immeasurable value and drop it into the deepest part of the ocean, where it can never be found again.

Deciding you want to break your agreement is a

necessary step, but if you absolutely want to change a belief it can't be done by thinking or affirmation alone. Remember, the intellect retrieves information from your library of knowledge, applies it to the situation at hand, and the Interpreter expresses what you have come to believe. You don't believe what you think; you think what you believe.

The attachment to what you believe is often way too strong to be broken just by saying to yourself, "I'm done with this. I want to stop." Obsessive or addictive behavior like overeating or smoking is rarely changed by putting a sign on your refrigerator stating, *I'm thin,* or *I'm smoke free.* Behavior is the belief expressing itself and cannot be changed simply by changing your mind. What drives your behavior is not what you think but what you actually believe.

Really letting go of something is a lot like true forgiveness. Consider the act of forgiveness. Are there people whom you have not forgiven? Are there things you have done that you have not forgiven yourself for? Why not?

Often, we just can't forgive. Although we may want to completely let it go, the debate in our minds and the emotion tied to the event are too strong, especially when the offense has occurred repeatedly over a long period of time. Our insistence on not forgiving and the arguments that support that position become a jewel of immeasurable value. The attachment is very powerful, much like the tale of Gollum from the book trilogy *The Lord of the Rings,* and his addiction to his "precious"—the One Ring.

Listen to the discussion in your mind when you don't forgive, when you can't let it go. It's all about what you did and what they did. Who should have done this or who should have done that. Who's right and who's wrong. It sounds like an argument. It sounds like a lawyer arguing a case.

When lawyers come before the judge to plead a case, they provide evidence, cite precedent, and present an argument with one specific goal in mind. They are there to prove they are right. If you listen to what you say to yourself when you think about someone you can't forgive, what you hear is an argument about being right. You can't forgive because you need to be right.

The reason we can't let go of what we have come to believe—even if it is no longer serving us, even if we now disagree—is because we are the champion of that point of view and will defend it at every turn. We need to be right.

Have you ever listened to someone complain that what they really want is impossible to get? If you listen closely to what they are saying, they will present all sorts of evidence to prove their point. If you suggest another way of looking at it they will likely respond, "Yes, I hear what you are saying . . . but."

The *Yes, . . . but* indicates they are addicted to their need to be right.

In order to let go of an agreement you have made that has been reinforced thousands of times—that has your attention, hooks your mind with its point of view, and has an emotional perspective that is both powerful and overwhelming—give up the need to be right. Giving up the need to be right stops every avenue where the belief is expressing itself. It suspends justification and evidence gathering, blocking the primary source of nourishment—you. Deciding to give up the need to be right is not just a thought but a far-reaching action that releases your investment of faith. Faith in what you believe.

Giving up the need to be right does not mean what you observe isn't accurate. You just give up your interpretation, because that's where the attachment is to being right.

As an example, suppose you see a homeless man on the street. He appears to be sick and doesn't seem to have much energy. His clothes are torn and tattered. He looks dirty, as if he hasn't bathed in a long time. In your mind you may start to think about how you might help him. Maybe you can even save him from whatever has gotten him to this place. Perhaps you start thinking about how this person is lazy, and if he just got a job like everyone else he wouldn't have to live on the street. Maybe you are disgusted by anyone who would let themselves get into such sorry shape.

What you notice about the homeless man and the condition he's in is most likely correct. The rest of it is your assessment, your interpretation. Whether you are going to be the hero, the social worker, or the reformer is all about the need to be right.

Everybody defends their point of view. Nobody likes to be made wrong so why give up your need to be right? It's such an integral part of our culture. We are trained from a young age to be right. Being right is a way to be accepted. Editorials; call-in shows; court room battles; terrorism; debates in coffee shops, classrooms, and the bedroom all touch on the need to be right. You could try to convince yourself that you should give up your need to be right because of some moral argument about forgiveness or because it sounds like a reasonable thing to do. For me, there is only one solid reason to give up the need to be right. Because it feels good.

Years ago I went on a trip to the Inca ruins at Machu Picchu in Peru with don Miguel. One day he asked me, "Why am I here?"

I thought about it and I said, "To teach us."

"Nope," he replied. "Wrong answer."

I thought about it some more and said, "To change the world."

"Nope," he replied. "Wrong answer." He was in a particularly feisty mood that day and although I had several clever answers come into my mind, part of me knew I was still headed in the wrong direction.

"Okay," I said, "tell me. Why are you here?"

"For pleasure," he replied.

It took me years to understand what he meant. At first, I thought it was about physical pleasure, like getting a massage or lounging in a hot tub and sipping fine wine.

What I began to understand was that he deliberately acted in certain ways because of the emotion it invoked—because it felt pleasurable to him. He loved to play, laugh, and have fun. No matter what kind of exchange I had with him, there was always a sense he was meeting me with kindness, respect, and love without conditions. So I tried it too. The emotion tied to treating myself and others with respect, kindness, and love was highly pleasurable. Learning to stop the world, turning off my mind and riding moment to moment in a sensation of feelings with no words to describe it, was delightful. Somehow, merging with nature, breathing it and allowing it to breathe me was exquisite. I learned when I aligned my attention and intention with the creative power of love without limits I felt tremendous pleasure.

Giving up the need to be right is like that. One compelling reason to give up the need to be right is pleasure. If you take the time to notice how you feel when you take any action, without using words to define your perception, you may discover that emotions advise directly based on how it feels.

The action of giving up the need to be right allows

your attachment to the viewpoint of the belief to crumble, igniting an emotion that is simply delight-ful.

To completely let go of an old belief that is no longer serving you, give up the need to be right.

Chapter 7

THE THIRD STEP:
LOVE WITHOUT LIMITS

As you learn to practice awareness, learn
to practice kindness. Kindness for yourself.
Treat yourself with kindness, respect, and
love without limits when considering all the
decisions you have made up till now—even
the foolish ones.

The third step in changing a belief
requires that you treat yourself with
love. Real love. Real love is love with-
out limits—love without conditions. Treating yourself
with love without limits is completely accepting yourself, as you are, despite any conversation in your
mind about how you *should* be or what you *should*
have done.

Most of us know about love with conditions. We
can love if the right conditions are met, and if we love
then we expect something back. Love with conditions

is an agreement that implies, *If you act this way then I will love you. I will love you if . . .* In that agreement it is safe to love. It applies not only to everyone around you but to the way you treat yourself as well.

In the First Dream we learned what love is. When you were a child did you ever knock over a glass of milk or drop a dish of food on the floor? Maybe one or both of your parents became upset. *Look at what you have done! What's wrong with you? Why can't you be more careful? When will you learn to pay attention?* They were upset and it seemed to be your fault. You did something wrong and now they didn't appear to love you like before.

Sometimes, in a situation like that, we decide it's up to us to make it better. We have to modify our behavior and try some strategy to get them to love us again. Or maybe we react, becoming irritated by what happened and their response to it. *It was an accident. I didn't do anything wrong. I can't understand why they are so upset with me. What is their problem?* We are agitated by their behavior and they need to be different before we can love them again.

These two responses arise from exactly the same agreement. It just depends whether we have a predilection for pointing the finger inwardly at ourselves or outwardly toward everyone else.

The drama around knocking over the glass of milk, or something like it, happens thousands of times in hundreds of different ways on the path to now. We learn we are not okay as we are or decide they are not okay as they are. We learn that giving and getting love is a game. A game of punishment and reward.

The rules of the game demand that when you, or someone else, does something wrong you are guilty, need to be punished, and should be ashamed. When you are a "good girl" or a "good boy," you get the prize. The prize of love and acceptance.

In the First Dream, there are two basic rules about getting or giving love:

 ⟡ Love and acceptance is a commodity that exists outside of me, and to get it I have to say the right thing, do the right thing, and be the right thing.

 ⟡ I am responsible for others' emotions and happiness and in turn, they are responsible for mine. If they react in a negative way to something I do or say, I need to be different so they will be happy. However, if they do or say something that upsets me then it's their fault, and they need to behave in a different way before I can be happy.

As we become adults the Voices of the First Dream use this definition of what love is from our book of rules to judge everyone, including ourselves. The book of rules defines a standard of how to act and how to feel. If your book of rules says, *Negative emotions are not okay in me or in others,* then when you become upset you might think, "I shouldn't feel this way. I need to fix it." You decide you are not okay as you are and you need in some way to be different.

In the same way, if you discover you have done things in the past you now judge as not good enough, then according to the first rule—*To get love and acceptance I have to say the right thing, do the right thing, and be the right thing*—you can't accept yourself as you are. If you can't accept yourself as you are, then you have decided the part of you that made mistakes in the past is not worthy of being loved.

The definition of what love is, from your book of rules, comes right into play when you begin to have real awareness about a belief you determine has been holding you back or has created unnecessary drama in your life. When you become acutely aware of what a fearful belief has produced over the years, you might say to yourself, "Oh my—what have I done? How could I have been so blind?" Once you wake up to how deep it goes and how many layers there are, you may find a new theme for *I'm Not.* A whole new place of—*I'm not doing it right. I should have known better. I've wasted so much time. I should have realized this years ago, and now I'm out of time.* If the perspective of the belief has caused you emotional pain, it is likely you will decide it's a problem and needs to be fixed. The awareness of the belief, what it has created in your life, and the rejection of the emotions attached to it become just another way you decide you're not okay as you are.

Holding on to the point of view—*I should have known better. I've wasted so much time. I should have realized this years ago*—is about needing to be right. Hashing it over and over in your mind, obsessing about what has happened and what you should have done keeps you stuck in the role of defender of the belief despite your intent to change it.

In order to practice love without limits, we need to know what real love is. There are over thirty words in the English language alone related to the concept of love. And most of them have to do with romantic love. Is our notion of romantic love really love? And how does the sentiment of love apply outside of romance, like loving your family, your pet, your work, and most importantly, yourself?

The concept of love from The First Dream is not love at all. It's fear.

Because love is so hard to pin down with words and can be confusing to apply, the easiest way to recognize it is to know what it is not. What love is not is something we are infinitely familiar with and can identify with no misunderstanding. Fear. Not the natural fear that keeps you from getting hurt physically, but unreasonable fear. Fear that makes you suffer. Fear based on lies.

The simplest definition of love is *not-fear*. In just the same way, fear is *not-love*.

There is a simple litmus test. In whatever situation you are in, no matter what decision you need to make, listen to the dialog you have around it. Look at all the arguments and points of view. Ask yourself one simple question. Is this fear, or is this not-fear?

Love is a force—a living perspective that can be applied to everything in your life. Moment to moment. Day in and day out. Understanding love without limits doesn't take a lot of effort or intellectual prowess. Love without limits is simply the act of deliberately taking a point of view that serves only one master. Not-fear.

What is really true is that in every moment of your life you have done the best you could. As much as the Demon of Perfection argues to the contrary, it is not possible in the moments that have passed you could have done any better. You get it when you get it. You realize something the minute you realize it and not one minute before.

If you are dedicated to ongoing growth, self-improvement, and your own personal excellence, then saying, "I did the best I could at the time" is not an excuse, but recognition that the Demon of Perfection is a liar. If you want to feel better and learn from the actions that haven't given you the results you want, being overly critical of yourself and dwelling on what you should have done won't help and actually supports the agreements you are trying to break.

Loving yourself without limits is about taking care of yourself the same way you would take care of someone you love deeply. Loving yourself without limits is treating yourself to the kind of love a mother gives her little one, regardless of the mischief they have gotten into that day.

Love in The First Dream is love for a reason. *I will love you if . . . I will love you when . . .* Love without limits is love for no reason at all. Love without limits is a decision based simply on the way it feels.

When you discover an agreement that now seems foolish to you, it is normal to feel like a fool. No matter what it is you have created for yourself, you have done the best you could up to this point. Give up punishing yourself because you should have known better. Stop rejecting yourself because some of the emotions tied to what you have come to believe aren't the way you would like them to be. Give up the need to be right about how you think it should have been. As you learn to practice awareness, learn to practice kindness. Kindness for yourself. Treat yourself with kindness, respect, and love without limits when considering all the decisions you have made up till now—even the foolish ones.

Each step in changing a belief ties into the next one. Changing a belief starts by becoming acutely aware of it and getting so fed up you decide to break the vows, oaths, and promises you have made with yourself—withdrawing your investment of faith. Changing a belief is about giving up your need to be right—even about being right that you should have done it differently. Finally, changing a belief requires love without limits. Releasing your investment of faith in the idea you should have realized all this long ago is an act of forgiveness only possible when you choose love. Loving yourself without limits is knowing you have always done the best you could in the moments that have passed. Love without limits is loving yourself so much that you treat yourself with kindness, respect, and not-fear, no matter what. It takes all that to release the old belief—a powerful living dream.

Chapter 8

THE FINAL STEP:
CREATE A NEW DREAM

In order to begin to fabricate The Second Dream you choose—for a second time—where to place your attention and what to believe. To do this takes understanding what you have come to believe, releasing the old beliefs that are holding you back, and designing new beliefs that support the life you want.

The first three steps to change a belief—practicing awareness, giving up the need to be right, and loving yourself without limits—are required to release the old agreement. The fourth and final step is about taking action to reconstruct the belief, and this can only be done by using the same elements and dynamics that created it in the first place.

We all possess the natural elements of human perception. These are the *Tools of Perception*—

emotion; the physical senses of sight, taste, touch, hearing, and smell; as well as the focus and discernment of our awareness, our attention. The Tools of Perception are an integral part of us, the integrity of the human being. It is through the Tools of Perception that we perceive the world and continually assemble and modify our filter of belief.

Your personal belief system, designed in The First Dream, was constructed by choosing where to focus your attention, establishing channels of communication through the Tools of Perception, and making agreements by investing your faith and energy over time. Right now, as in every moment, it is your interpretation through this filter of belief that creates your version of what is real—your personal Island of the Known.

There are billions of human beings on the planet, each with their own unique virtual reality. Strong opinions about how we should act are lodged in ideologies about government, religion, economics, spirituality, and so much more. We are bombarded by media—radio, TV, print, and the Internet—all vying for our attention. Every group, whether it be a country, a town, a corporation, a trade organization, or the family next door, has a distinct point of view that is apparent when we are in the sphere of their influence. Each person, each group, contributes to the collective mind of the human beings that is dreaming all the time. Each time we focus our attention on any portion of that dream, we plug into whatever is being communicated. Without awareness we eat with our perception what is being broadcast simply by allowing our attention to be hooked.

In every moment, aware or not, you decide where to focus your attention. Moment to moment you put your attention on something—an object, a sound, a picture, someone talking, or a thought. Wherever you place your attention, if there is any sort of an agreement, a channel of communication is opened and meaning is received. When you establish a channel of communication with your attention, your filter of belief distorts the input, and at the same time what comes through the channel is modifying your personal dream.

Noticing the dynamic of The First Dream and deliberately choosing where to put your attention, choosing what to agree to, choosing what to consume with your awareness begin what the Toltecs called "The Dream of the Second Attention" or what I will call "The Second Dream." When you intend to change a belief you consciously direct your own attention for a second time. In The First Dream your beliefs are in control of your attention. In The Second Dream your attention begins to control your beliefs.

In order to begin to fabricate The Second Dream, you choose, for a second time, where to place your attention and what to believe. To do this takes understanding what you have come to believe, releasing the old beliefs that are not serving you, and creating new beliefs that support the life you want.

The final step to changing a belief starts with choosing a new agreement that reworks the belief you want to modify.

One of my coaching clients, Jeff, had a pattern of acting reserved and guarded. He was intently focused on doing everything just right. Before he went to meetings at work, he would rehearse in his mind all the possible conversations that might occur so he would say the right thing at the right moment. He would go to parties and try to blend in with whatever was happening in the room, but shortly after he arrived he would become uncomfortable and feel like he didn't belong. Dating made him very nervous because he was so focused on his performance being perfect. It was impossible for him to relax and just be himself.

Jeff had come to me with the goal of jump-starting his career. It was easy to see how his pattern of behavior was holding him back, not only at his job, but in his personal relationships as well.

As a result of our work, he became aware of an agreement underneath his behavior. Through the opinions of the adults that had been impressed upon him in The First Dream, he had agreed to the idea that no one would accept him just the way he was. He discovered he had adopted the first rule of getting love: *Love and acceptance is a commodity that exists outside of me. To get it, I have to say the right thing, do the right thing, and be the right thing.* He was so afraid he would do it wrong, it almost paralyzed him. His reserved and guarded behavior was a mask covering intense anxiety. He had an overwhelming fear of being found out because what he really believed was there wasn't any way he could do it right.

To change his belief, he started by mapping out a new agreement he would make with himself: *First, I agree to like myself. Next, I agree the approval, acceptance, and love I want begins with me. I agree to treat myself with kindness, respect, and love without limits regardless of anyone else's opinion about who I am or what I should do. I have goals I want to achieve both in myself and out in the world. Without question, I want to improve in the days to come, but in all the moments that have passed I accept I have done the best I could.*

Identifying your new agreement is a powerful first step. Write it down. This may sound simple, but real transformation occurs when an idea is written down on paper. Until you write it down, it's merely a thought that may evaporate as easily as your dreams do when you wake up in the morning.

Next, begin to practice it. Remember that you have, over a long period of time and through lots of effort, mastered the old belief. To master anything you must practice it.

I live in the Rocky Mountains of Colorado and have recently renewed my interest in skiing. I love watching skiers who come down the mountain effortlessly with seemingly perfect form. It's also frustrating because I'm trying to remember all the little nuances and I struggle to execute the simplest things. When I talk about my process to people who ski well, I hear the same thing over and over again. It takes time and practice before the body remembers and executes without having to try so hard.

Belief does not change overnight, but rather the new agreement gains momentum each time you choose it. In The First Dream, what you believe controls your attention. It has power because you bestowed it with power. It has control because you agreed. In just the same way, each time you invest yourself in a new belief the balance of power shifts. Each time you take action and choose the new agreement you have made, the domination of the old viewpoint recedes.

The next thing you can do to reinforce a belief is create a new story and gather evidence to support that story.

Little children make up stories to help organize the events, actions, and feelings of each day. Many little ones, after they are put down for a nap or go to bed, talk themselves to sleep. As young as two, they use storytelling to make decisions and agreements about what is happening to them. Storytelling is a natural part of our development resulting in the beliefs, oaths, and promises that later dominate our attention. To redesign any belief, drop the old story, tell a different story, and assemble evidence to strengthen your new story.

You have been very successful establishing that your old story is correct by gathering evidence to prove you are right. A new belief is just a new story. If you want to adopt beliefs that enhance and nurture a new dream of life, start by looking for evidence that supports those beliefs.

Once you have recovered your faith, to create a new belief you have to reinvest your faith. Evidence gathering is a powerful way to do that. If you want to change what you believe, gather different evidence. Use this dynamic to sustain beliefs that foster happiness and personal excellence rather than a device to create drama. Make evidence gathering your ally. Notice and catalogue when you get praise for your performance. Recognize when something turns out exceptionally well. Make a habit of honoring and accentuating all the events that support what you are trying to create as your new personal agreement. Start collecting different evidence.

Another way to strengthen a belief is to imagine its perspective. Because we are a product of what we experience, you'd expect that to begin to believe something you have to experience it over and over again. For example, to become a skilled tennis player you need a lot of experience playing tennis and succeeding at it. But is that all? No. You have to decide you are capable of it. In some way you have to agree you are it before you can become it, even if it isn't true . . . yet.

Have you ever heard the story of the four-minute mile? For many years people believed it was impossible for any human being to run a mile in less than four minutes. Roger Bannister, an English physician and middle distance runner, broke the four-minute barrier in May of 1954. Bannister believed it was possible, imagined it, and used his knowledge as a physician to his advantage. He painstakingly researched the mechanical aspects of running and developed scientific training methods to aid him in achieving his goal.

Within one year after Bannister shattered the belief barrier, 37 runners broke the four-minute mark. The year after that, 300 other runners did the very same thing. We become capable of achieving anything the moment we decide it's possible.

For years, athletes have used visualization techniques to enhance their performance. They imagine themselves performing well at their sport repeatedly as if they are dreaming it. To a well-conditioned, well-trained athlete, belief is an important key to exceptional performance. To take on a new belief you don't have to wait until you experience it as a solid part of your life. You can begin to be *it* before it *is*. If you understand the results you want and the emotional point of view of the new belief as well, then you can dream it. If you can dream it and know how it feels as a point of reference, then, in that moment, you can *be* it. You can begin to be it before the result you want has completely manifested.

Working on the steps to change his belief, Jeff wrote down his new agreement and began to collect evidence to support it. In order to collect evidence, he reviewed his memory and wrote down all the moments he could remember where he had the experience of being loved, appreciated, self-confident, successful, and secure. He started there and used that as a point of reference. A point of reference, in this case, is just a memory that has an emotion to it. It's a living dream with a particular point of view. If you know how it feels, you can find your way back.

Next, he used the technique of imagining the perspective of the new belief. In order for him to use these memories as a point of reference, I instructed him to close his eyes and remember—to sense, to feel, and to dream. He imagined moments where he had the experience of being loved, appreciated, self-confident, successful, and secure until he could really feel it. He visualized this until he could be it. In his imagination he took this new point of view into the memory of being at a party where he was uncomfortable. He dreamed, while awake, being at the party with his new way of being—his new belief.

Another way to support your new agreement is to seek out someone who has real faith in the belief you want to adopt. Find a mentor for your new agreement.

Look for someone who is living, day to day, the point of view you want to create for yourself. You can find mentors in many ways. Go to meetings, gatherings, or conventions where people who are achieving what you want to accomplish are likely to gather. Just taking the action to go out and search for a mentor injects life into your belief redesign project, giving you new ideas and perspectives.

Once you identify a personal mentor, spend some time with them. Using the posture learned by becoming the Hunter of Beliefs, experience how they move through the world influenced by the beliefs you want for yourself. Maybe the life you've only dreamed of exists outside of your Island of the Known, but it probably exists inside someone else's Island of the Known. If you want to begin to experience the things you want that are not true for you right now, venture off the island. By experiencing the living dreams of people who believe what you'd like to believe, you will begin to definitively expand what you know.

An association with a mentor does not always have to be a one-to-one relationship. You can find the influence of mentors in books, movies, seminars, and articles. Whether they are famous or live just around the corner, their actions and accomplishments speak volumes about what they believe.

In addition to locating a mentor, consider engaging a coach. The desire to change what you believe is an intention that will assist you in identifying and reaching new goals. Goals that are specific, attainable, and measurable. If you want the support of someone who is trained to assist you in setting and achieving your goals, hire a coach.

Changing a belief takes time. Imagine you own a house but rent it out and let someone else manage it for you. One day you get a call from the manager letting you know that the neighbors are complaining about the people renting your house. When you go to check it out you find there are some pretty rough characters living there. The property is a mess. You tell your renters they must change their behavior or they will have to move out. A month later the neighbors call to complain again. When you go back to investigate, you find nothing has changed and so you ask your renters to leave. You tell them you cannot agree to them living in your house any longer. Finally they move out, but when you go back to inspect the house, you discover it's still a mess.

Changing a belief is a lot like that. At first, you really don't know what is going on. When you begin to gain awareness you negotiate with yourself hoping you don't have to make any big changes. Finally, when you stop tolerating the situation, you break the agreement. You say to the belief that has been residing with you for so long, *Get out of my house and take your stuff with you!* But even after the agreement is broken, there is still a lot of debris left by years of investment in the belief. It takes time and effort to put your house back in order. But that's not all. It takes courage.

When Jeff went to a party after designing his new agreement he had the goal of walking up to people he didn't know, being at ease, and starting up a conversation. He tried it and was still uncomfortable. He noticed the old script running in his head. It wasn't fun and it was difficult to relax. Although he wanted to give it up after the first few times, he didn't back down. That's because he had courage.

To have courage doesn't mean you don't have fear. The act of courage confronts and acknowledges fear. To have courage means to persist despite the fear. Embracing what challenges you means that your dedication to the goal is more important than rejection— that the accomplishment is more important than comfort. To have courage requires that you detach from any story about what might happen if you take action and willingly step away from your Island of the Known.

If Jeff went to the party, tried to connect with a stranger, and succumbed to the old script, that would be an act of agreement. Agreement with the old belief. By pushing past the fear, his action, because of his courage, was now an act of disagreement. His disagreement was an act of disobedience and restored his authority. Before, he had abdicated his authority to the old belief and bowed down to the fear.

To change a belief and step past the boundaries of

the Island of the Known requires not only courage but also commitment. But what is a commitment—the act of keeping your word? Saying you will do something and then doing it? It's more than that. True commitment is a Yes. In The First Dream, commitment is often a trap. True commitment is impeccable. It's a *Yes*—not just a sound that comes from your mouth— a complete promise that comes from the heart, the mind, and the spirit. A resounding Yes radiates from every fiber of your being.

Actually we are always saying yes, but we are hardly aware of it. It is more like surrender than an act of will. For example, a person who goes to work each day but can hardly stand their job has said yes. Not to the work, but to the idea it's all right to work 40 hours a week at something they can barely tolerate. Every agreement you make over time and through an investment of faith becomes a belief you have said yes to.

Changing habits and breaking old agreements is a process that takes you past the borders of your comfort zone—the Island of the Known. To make the journey requires passing through the *Gates of Change*, places where you go deeper into the next level of commitment. They are gates because this is where you meet the wall of your own fear and encounter resistance to pushing past what you know. To pass cleanly through the Gates of Change requires a commitment. It requires a Yes.

Many times when we are asked for a commitment we say yes with our mouth, but what we really mean is no or maybe. Have you ever been served in a restaurant, or at the checkout counter, by someone who never looks you in the eye and just goes through the motions? Have you ever watched a couple in a relationship where they seem to ignore each other and rarely connect except to argue? Most likely they are showing up but saying no with almost every part of their being. You can see it. You can feel it. When you say yes but don't mean it, you throttle the flow of possibility and stand frozen at the Gates of Change.

Sometimes what stops Yes and the commitment that follows is the idea that saying yes has a high cost. We think saying yes means we will be committed for a very long time, so we ride the fence with no more than a maybe. A true Yes is an impeccable action in the moment. Yes has no time frame. Whatever action you decide to take, no matter how routine, say Yes now. In the next moment, you can say no if that is what you choose.

Yes with all your will begets passion and authority. Real authority, not the cheap authority of someone who believes *I'm Not* telling someone else, *You're Not.* Yes is a choice made with the awareness and recognition that the exact result is an unknown. You can still say Yes, understanding that you can't control everything, you can't predict everything, and you can't with any certainty know exactly what will happen next.

Yes is an act of faith. Yes is a maneuver brimming with authority and passion. Yes throws open the Gates of Change and supercharges the act of creation.

To reweave the fabric of your belief past what you know, come to the Gates of Change, consider what you want, and if you choose to walk through, say Yes. Start on the journey even though you don't know where it is going to take you. See what happens when you choose to believe something else. Take action and say Yes!

You have always agreed where to put your attention, opening channels of communication that ultimately feed what you believe. Using the Tools of Perception, you have assembled your personal Island of the Known. With awareness you can now choose to believe what brings you pleasure, peace, power, purpose, and passion. When you change what you believe, your behavior changes. When you change what you believe, you change what you do. If belief is a living dream, then create a new dream. A new dream fueled by the Power of Belief!

Chapter 9

THE PROMISE OF ACCOUNTABILITY

Your intent is the mastery of your faith. Whether you are aware of it or not, by your faith you have gotten everything you have really asked for. You have invested your faith by agreement and now that is what you truly believe.

To change what we have created requires awareness, honesty, and accountability. In order to modify anything we need to become accountable for our part in creating it in the first place. How we process everything that has happened to us and the agreements we have made as a result was entirely based on choice. Things don't always go the way we want them to and sometimes they don't go well at all, but the decisions we make in those moments are what we have agreed to believe.

We think we are in control of so many things, but in fact we are not. All we have control over are where we place our attention and the decisions we make about what happens to us, or around us. All we have control over are the stories we tell about everything.

If we are truly accountable for the story we make up about what has happened to us, then we are not victims. As children, we are innocent and dependent. The adults are bigger, smarter, and stronger. There is no question about that, but the story of the Victim is that they still feel they have no choice. Victim self-talk: *It's not my fault, It's not fair and I can't help it,* is based on the point of view that it happened to me and I am powerless to change it, even now. If that is true, there is no hope at all . . . but it's not true.

There is hope, and it is in the *Promise of Accountability.* No matter what has happened to you, in your reaction to it you made an agreement and fabricated a story to support that agreement. At each juncture, you made a decision. Mindful or not, you said yes to a certain point of view.

Perhaps you have read about, or even know personally, someone who was in an accident and is now in a wheelchair paralyzed from the waist down. Some people who have had this happen to them live a life of bitterness and anger. Others take on the challenge and find a new dedication to expressing their enthusiasm and joy for life. What happens to us is sometimes out of our control, but we agree what to believe about it.

In every moment you choose where to put your

attention, whether you are aware of it or not. Your personal structure of belief has been assembled by choosing to focus your attention, establishing channels of communication, and making agreements—investing your faith and energy over time. You put lots of effort into constructing your own personal version of what is true. You create a big story about how things are and each time you retell it, you invest your faith in it.

Many times we don't recognize that the story we tell acts to abuse us. We don't notice that we frequently take on the role of the Victim. However, if we listen closely, any trace of complaining indicates the Victim is speaking. For the Victim, their story supports the place where they are stuck. *I can't. It's hopeless. I don't have any other choice. It's out of my control. I don't know what to do. It's her fault, it's his fault, it's their fault.*

If you want to know where you have invested your faith, listen to the stories you tell yourself and anyone who will listen. What is interesting is all the little details of the story that prove you are right are not that important. What is important is the belief behind it.

One spring I was in Austria teaching a seminar and I had set up some private coaching appointments. I had an appointment with a woman who only spoke German, so the interview was done with an interpreter present. The plan was that each person would speak a few sentences and then pause so the interpreter could translate. The woman was in her early fifties, nicely dressed, and had a pleasant smile. I had seen her husband the day before. She came in and said, "Everything is all right with me, but my husband thought it would be a good idea if I saw you." I asked her what she wanted. She ignored the question and talked about her husband and his problems. I asked her again, "What do you want?" She stared at me with a puzzled look on her face, and again talked about her husband's problems. I asked her the same question a third time. "What do *you* want?" She started to cry and began talking very quickly, barely pausing to take a breath. The interpreter stopped translating because she couldn't keep up.

I didn't understand what was being said, but I could see what was going on. Her facial expressions, her body language, and the tone and volume of her voice said it all. She was in her story. She launched her justification of why she was stuck and how it would never get any better. It wasn't important that I knew what the sounds coming out of her mouth meant. It was the point of view of her story that was significant. Her story supported the belief that she was hopelessly trapped. Her investment of faith declared: *This is the way it is and it will never change.*

Your intent is the mastery of your faith. Whether you are aware of it or not, by your faith you have gotten everything you have really asked for. You have invested your faith by agreement and now that is what you truly believe.

The Promise of Accountability says you have come to where you are because you made decisions. You have come to where you are because you agreed. You have come to where you are because you invested your faith. The Promise of Accountability is about recognizing all the actions you have taken to create and nurture the beliefs that are now obstacles to creating the life you want. The Promise of Accountability is good news and refutes the voice that states—*This is how it is, and I can't change.* If beliefs are created by focusing your attention, establishing a channel of communication, engaging all the Tools of Perception, making an agreement, collecting evidence, and then practicing that agreement until you have no doubt about it; there is no reason why you can't employ all of those strategies to build new beliefs—this time with awareness.

You have always had the power to choose something else. Something else to believe. Become accountable for all the agreements you have made up to now, and reinvest your faith consciously in beliefs that empower you. Take new action—action as a *not-victim.* Just this one decision can make all the difference in the world.

Chapter 10

I Am

> The real you—I Am—is your own inner fountain of inspiration, power, pleasure, and artistry.

The most powerful beliefs you can choose are the ones that rest on a solid foundation. The most solid foundation of all is the truth. The truth is that the belief, *I'm Not,* is a lie. Before we ever agree to believe *I'm Not,* it was someone else's opinion and probably someone else's opinion before that.

If we believe we are small and insignificant, or that we don't deserve abundance, or that we will never realize our most precious dreams, then we agree—*I'm Not.* If we play roles and wear masks to protect ourselves so we can't be seen, then we agree—*I'm Not.* If we accept the notion that persistent sadness about the past or constant anxiety about the future is normal, then we agree—*I'm Not.* Regardless of our accomplishments, if we capitulate to a life of little joy and don't believe we can achieve success in the full circle of living, then we agree—*I'm Not.*

Despite your problems or any drama in your life, the sun rises and sets every day. The seasons come and pass each year whether you are paying attention or not. As you are reading this your heart is beating and you have been breathing in and out, no matter what you believe about yourself and everything around you.

Regardless of what you have allowed yourself to believe, your authentic self shines like a bright star. It's always there and never goes out—an endless source of all things divine. An unlimited wellspring of delight and creativity. It's life itself. YOU are life itself. You and everyone who takes a breath are intimately connected to all living things and that which created them. Through this connection anything is possible. The real you—*I Am*—is your own inner fountain of inspiration, power, pleasure, and artistry.

Beyond the world created by what we believe, we are not separate from anything. We are a part of everything and everything is a part of us. The entire universe and everything in it are one presence that has magically and magnificently projected itself into billions of forms. Each of us is one of those forms and in the same moment the entire universe. To quote a well-worn cliché, you are a drop of water and at the same time the whole ocean. But we focus our attention on the drop, forgetting the ocean. In an act of magnificent self-importance we define ourselves by our image, our story, and the pressure of our daily lives. Because of what we believe, we can't see past the Island of the Known, yet at the deepest level we are unbounded. We are the life experiencing itself through the human body, thought, and emotion. We are the art of the creator. We are *I Am.*

The Voices of the First Dream—the Judge, the Victim, and the Prostitute—are teachers that lead us to *I Am.* Once redeemed, the Victim teaches us about our own personal power and authority. The Judge teaches us about justice and truth tempered by love. The Prostitute teaches us about self-love, respect, and faith. Each voice of The First Dream confronted becomes an ally.

When we allow the story we tell about ourselves and everything around us to collapse—in that moment everything is all right as it is. Once the road of *I'm Not* is no longer tended, natural forces will heave the road. Withdrawing our investment of faith in *I'm Not* reveals what is, without effort. *I Am.*

I Am okay. *I Am* good enough. *I Am* capable. *I Am* in this moment, perfect. *I Am* peace. *I Am* able to love myself without limits. *I Am* human. *I Am* Divine, as is all the creation I see around me.

Allowing yourself to invest your faith in *I Am* reveals the true power of belief.

You are *I Am.*

Part III

Tools

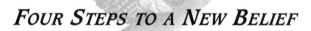

FOUR STEPS TO A NEW BELIEF

THE FIRST STEP

Practice Awareness

To transform any belief takes awareness. Awareness of what you really believe. In the process of changing a belief, developing a habit of aware-ness is most of the task—per-haps 90 percent of the journey. Reclaiming your awareness opens a whole universe of pos-sibility; a new beginning of building beliefs that support a life you can love. In order to recover your awareness, prac-tice awareness.

In Order to Practice Awareness

Step off your Island of the Known

Track your reactions as the Hunter of Beliefs

Disagree with the Voices of The First Dream

Ask the Questions of Disbelief

Silence the Interpreter

THE SECOND STEP

Give up the Need to Be Right

To let go of any belief that no longer serves you, give up the need to be right. Giving up the need to be right suspends justification and evidence gathering, blocking the primary source of nourishment—you. Giving up the need to be right is a far-reaching action releasing your investment of faith. Faith in what you believe.

In Order to Give up the Need to Be Right

Use your new habit of awareness to notice when you need to be right

Observe how being right feels and let the emotion guide you

Stop collecting evidence that supports the old belief

Disregard the storyteller

THE THIRD STEP

Love Yourself without Limits

When you discover an old belief that now seems foolish to you, it is normal to feel like a fool. No matter what you have created for yourself up to this point, you have done the best you could. Treat yourself with kindness, respect, and love without limits when considering all the decisions you have made up till now—even the foolish ones.

In Order to
Love Yourself without Limits

Give up the need to be right

Stop practicing love according to
The First Dream

Embrace the act of forgiveness

Reject the Demon of Perfection

Ask the question:
Is this fear or not-fear?

THE FINAL STEP

Create a New Dream

Belief is a living dream. To fabricate a new dream, understand what you have come to believe, release any beliefs that are holding you back, and design new beliefs that support what you want to create. This final step is about taking action to reconstruct any limiting beliefs, and this can only be done by using the same elements and dynamics that created them in the first place.

In Order to Create a New Belief

Design a new agreement that re-works the old belief

Make up a new story and gather evidence to support it

Imagine it, dream it and be it— even before it is

Find a mentor for your new agreement

Charge through the Gates of Change with a Yes!

Gather your courage and push past the obstacles

DEFINITIONS

Hunter of Beliefs

The posture of awareness—not caught up in the action, but observing the action. Perception by watching, feeling, and listening without the Interpreter always explaining what you are seeing right in front of your eyes. The Hunter of Beliefs tracks the expression of any agreement that is not serving you, holding you back, or keeping you from having the life you want.

I Am

An endless source of all things divine. The real you—an expression intimately connected to all living things and that which created it. An infinite inner fountain of love, inspiration, power, delight, and artistry.

I'm Not

The belief passed down from the authors of The First Dream that you are not okay as you are, you are not enough, and no matter what, you never will be. *I'm Not* implies that you are not adequate, and to get love and acceptance you have to say the right thing, do the right thing, and be the right thing. Love is a conditional agreement that suggests, "I will love you if . . ." In that agreement love is always found outside of you, and getting the prize of acceptance is a game of punishment and reward officiated by your own inner judge.

Island of the Known

Your own personal island of safety constructed of your beliefs, other people's opinions, all your knowledge, concepts, and experiences. It is the result of what you have agreed to and invested your faith in. It is the container of "me" bounded by what you believe.

Lucid Living

The practice of becoming aware while you are awake that you are dreaming all the time, distorting what you perceive through the lens of your beliefs.

Promise of Accountability

How you process everything that has happened to you and the agreements you make is the result of your decisions. The Promise of Accountability says you have come to where you are because you agreed and thus invested your faith. You have always had the power to choose something else. Something else to believe.

Questions of Disbelief

Not completely accepting everything you think, everything you say, or what anyone else says. The Questions of Disbelief—*What just happened here? How do I feel? What am I telling myself? Is what I'm saying to myself absolutely true?*—breaks the spell of being completely convinced that you are the Interpreter living on the Island of the Known and nothing more.

The Book of Rules

The law your inner judge uses to pass judgment on you and everyone else around you. The book of rules is your book of judgment.

The Broken Heart

Unavoidably and without exception certain parts of your personal construction—the Island of the Known—fall apart. What has become your foundation shifts, causing the structure you have built to collapse. Eventually you adapt because you have to. You need to function and so you develop strategies to make you safe again. You rebuild, this time making your structure of belief more rigid, keeping you from living openly with real passion.

The Demon of Perfection

The inner judge says, "No matter what you do, no matter what you achieve, no matter how good it gets, it will *never* be good enough." This applies to you and is projected to everyone whose image appears in your virtual reality.

The First Dream

In order to pass information onto us when we were children, the adults needed to constantly capture our attention. In this way they taught us language. Once we understood the code, they could tell us about everything they knew. This process of capturing our attention for the first time creates, by agreement, our initial dream of how the world is.

The First Heartbreak

Small children have a natural unspoken agreement with their parents—*I can be myself, and you will love me unconditionally. You will protect me, and I'm safe with you. I can trust you, and you will take care of me. I can count on you to be there for me.* Invariably that agreement is broken many times.

The Gates of Change

Changing a belief and breaking old agreements is a process that takes you past the borders of your boundary of safety—the Island of the Known. To make the journey requires passing through the Gates of Change, places where you go deeper into the next level of commitment. They are gates because this is where you meet the wall of your own fear, and encounter resistance trying to push past what you know.

The Interpreter

The dominant dreamer of our life with a distinct point of view always telling us how everything is. The Interpreter uses all our knowledge and experience as a library to find evidence to support its personal description of the world. The gatekeeper of perception.

The Second Dream

Taking the reins and recovering your own attention begins The Second Dream. When you intend to change a belief developed in The First Dream, you focus your awareness—your attention—for the second time by choice. In The First Dream your beliefs control your attention. In The Second Dream your attention begins to control your beliefs.

Toltec

An ancient culture that thrived in what is now the pyramid ruins of Teotihuacán in the high midlands of Mexico. In a tradition that dates back thousands of years and continues today, the Toltec were known throughout Mexico as men and women of knowledge. They taught that there's no way for us to change unless we have an awareness of how we create our unique perception of the world. The Toltec description of the human being is that the mind is alive, and one of its main purposes is to dream. They concluded we are dreaming 24 hours a day and what we dream through is the filter of our beliefs about everything.

Tools of Perception

All the natural elements of human perception—emotion; the physical senses of sight, taste, touch, hearing, and smell; as well as the focus and discernment of our awareness, our attention. The Tools of Perception are an integral part of us, the integrity of the human being. It is through the Tools of Perception that we perceive the world and construct our filter of belief.

Voices of the First Dream

The Voices of the First Dream are outlets for beliefs that define the boundaries of the Island of the Known. Limiting beliefs often express a common agreement. I Can't and I'm Not. These inner voices expressing beliefs born in fear belong to various archetypal personalities including the Judge, the Victim, the Prostitute, the Hero, the Rescuer, and many more—all expressing a common theme.

Yes

An impeccable commitment. Not just a sound that comes from your mouth, but a total promise that comes from the heart, the mind, and the spirit. A resounding Yes emanating from every fiber of your being. Yes carries authority and passion. Yes throws open the Gates of Change and supercharges the act of creation.

Stop the World

Each day rushes on with more to do than there is time to do it. A perpetual merry-go-round that never stops so you can get off. What would happen if you suddenly stopped the world—even for just a few moments? Better yet, what would happen if you stopped your personal interpretation of everything, allowing yourself to observe the world without your habitual lens of belief? What you might see is a new world of possibility without the story. Your story.

To stop the world is to practice awareness, and for just a moment, surrender your description of everything that keeps your attention occupied.

Sit someplace quietly where there isn't anyone around to disturb you. Somewhere you feel safe. Take off your shoes. Sit up straight. Don't cross your legs. Rest your hands on your thighs. Get comfortable and then don't move! When you shift your body, you give away your will.

Your inner dialog has your attention much of the

time and so when you sit down to be still, there will be a war for your attention. Your mind will suggest that you fidget, scratch, or get up and write a note about something you might forget. To strengthen your will, don't move at all.

Just breathe. Slowly. Follow your breath with your attention. Breathe in through your nose slowly, imagining you are pulling air in from all over your body. Breathe out through your mouth, making the sound of the ocean or the wind. The in-breath is the will deliberately directing your attention as choice. The out-breath is letting go. Releasing everything.

As you breathe in let your body expand. As you breathe out let your awareness expand. Notice how you feel, in your emotions and in your body. Resist the temptation to describe this to yourself in words. Just be aware with no attempt to define it or explain it.

Start by practicing 15 minutes each day, several times a week. Exercise this new habit. If you lose your attention to the chatter in your mind, don't make yourself wrong. Just refocus. Find the space between the thoughts. Be kind to yourself. There is no such thing as doing it *right*.

ABOUT THE AUTHOR

Ray Dodd is a master belief coach, teacher, and Toltec wisdom mentor. As the founder of Everyday Wisdom, he helps both individuals and businesses forge new beliefs and agreements to effect lasting and positive change. Before becoming an author and coach, he was a professional musician, an engineer, and a corporate executive for a nationwide facilities company with more than one billion dollars in annual sales.

In addition to his coaching practice, he teaches seminars about Toltec wisdom and the Power of Belief throughout the United States and abroad.

If you would like Ray Dodd to speak at your next public event, association conference, or corporate meeting, please contact us at: info@everydaywisdom.us

EVERYDAY WISDOM

Everyday Wisdom is a group dedicated to helping individuals, organizations, and workplace groups identify the beliefs and agreements that present barriers to getting the results they want. Everyday Wisdom provides coaching, training, and intensive programs designed to change limiting beliefs, unleashing the potential for profound personal and workplace transformation.

If you'd like more information about one-to-one coaching, seminars, classes, programs for the workplace, or having Ray speak at a conference or event, please contact us at:

E-MAIL: info@everydaywisdom.us

WEB SITE: www.everydaywisdom.us

TOPICS FOR TALKS INCLUDE:

✧ The Power of Belief and Extraordinary
    Leadership

✧ The Power of Belief at Work
(Tools for Transforming the Way We Work)

✧ Real Communication
(Connecting Through Awareness)

✧ Make Better Decisions
(A New Approach to Taking Action)

✧ The Power of Belief in Love
(New Agreements for Relationship)

"Freedom"

by

DIANE DANDENEAU

To purchase prints of the cover or other works, please visit:

DIANE DANDENEAU STUDIOS

www.dandeneau.com

for a brochure call 800-823-4304

ACKNOWLEDGMENTS

To Susan Marshall and Noah Dodd, whose love, support, and belief in me have been the greatest gifts of all.

My heartfelt gratitude to all my teachers. There have been so many over the years I can't recall everyone. To the teachers who were in my life for a while and to those who only crossed my path for a moment in time, I thank you. Without any limit to my appreciation for his hand in my transformation, I thank don Miguel Ruiz. In addition, I wish to thank Gini Gentry (La Doña), Barbara Emrys, Allan Hardman, and Victoria Miller for their guidance.

A special thanks to Suzanne Bastear, whose imagination and loving hands created the concept for the cover of this book—and to Simeon Hein for inspiring me to keep going.

Another special thanks to Bob Friedman and all the wonderful folks at Hampton Roads Publishing for their vision and talent in bringing this all together.

Finally, my love and gratitude to all those who-have supported this work over the years and who were each, in some way, instrumental in developing the ideas found in this book. A partial list includes: Maru Ahumada, Alison Barrows, Beverly Beniot, Lanex Brink, Maggie Caffery, Fred Dearborn, David Dibble, Mitchell Dozor, Samie Dozor, Hal Foreman, Ed Fox, Thomas Gruner, Kim Gustafson, C. J. Hall, Marianne Heindl, Judy Herreid, Simeon Hein, Ron Jones, Camille King, Donna Krebs, Kit Kyle, Dawn Link, Christine Magdalene, Brad Meyers, Colleen Miller, Thomas Miller, Brandt Morgan, Darryl Morgan, Cynthia Morris, Sabine Mueller, Dr. Gene Nathan, Wendy Newman, Robin Nicolaus, Jeff Offsanko, Emily Palko, Massimo Perucchini, Peggy Raess, Susyn Reeve, Rita Rivera, Stewart Sallo, Eric Sanderson, Birgit Schwarz, Barbara Simon, Sandy Shipp, Shelly Steig, Joanna Strang, Mark Wergin, and Teresa Wergin.

Hampton Roads Publishing Company
. . . for the evolving human spirit

Hampton Roads Publishing Company
publishes books on a variety of subjects including
metaphysics, health, visionary fiction,
and other related topics.

For a copy of our latest catalog,
call toll-free, 800-766-8009,
or send your name and address to:

Hampton Roads Publishing Company, Inc.
1125 Stoney Ridge Road
Charlottesville, VA 22902

e-mail: hrpc@hrpub.com
www.hrpub.com